PORTUGAL

PORTUGAL

RECIPES & INGREDIENTS

Anaïs Bourny Delon

Photographs by Nicolas Lobbestaël

MITCHELL BEAZLEY

INTRODUCTION

This book is a journey through Portuguese food and the people behind it. It is a tribute to the culinary traditions of Portugal, the nation's cooks and artisans, both new and more established stars.

I want to introduce you to the Portugal of today, which is a blend of tradition and modernity. This book is not a collection of old family recipes, nor is it an exhaustive guide to the nation's cooking. Instead, it's a window on the best the country has to offer, the unique, the richest, brightest, most talented and vibrant Portuguese food.

To guide you on the way, I've included some traditional recipes, as well as lots of others that have been given a new spin, along with the country's latest food trends, tips from Portuguese chefs and the secrets of where to find the very best ingredients.

My own journey through the country's food began in spring 2018, when I set out to uncover rising stars from the west of the Iberian peninsula. I wanted to identify the best ambassadors for Portuguese cooking, past and present. Of course, the search for talent, chefs, products and producers also meant I made some totally unexpected discoveries. So come with me – and our photographer Nicolas – on a quirky, and sometimes surprising, gastronomic tour.

To kick off this journey to the heart of Portugal, I'd like to tell you about some of the people – the greatest living signposts who guided me through the food landscape – who I met along the way.

FROM AN UNLIKELY BEGINNING ...

My journey began in Paris, where I live and work. It was here that I met the cheerful, open-hearted Portuguese chef César De Sousa and visited his restaurant, which goes by the sweet, sing-song name of Pássarito (see pages 33 and 295), meaning 'little bird'. César is passionate, exciting and dynamic, and has a deep understanding of his country's cuisine and food culture. He quickly brought me up to speed, helping me to understand the most important dishes in Portugal's home cooking tradition: *caldo verde* soup, little *bifanas* sandwiches, octopus salads and, in particular, the hundreds of variations on salt cod: the beloved *bacalhau*. I listened attentively as he fed me details about the best places to discover in Lisbon and amazed me with the collection of organic Portuguese wines from his restaurant's cellar. César is a generous man who boasts good-humouredly, and with a pronounced accent, about his home country's beautiful recipes and stories. These are what have earned Portugal a place of honour internationally – particularly for the sunshine flavours of its seafood cookery – and for its long-standing food traditions that have been exported all over the world, since the time of the Crusades.

Once I'd tasted César's amazing food, as soon as I could I headed for Portugal's capital: Lisbon. It's a city that dances to its own rhythm. A city that's changing, but which has preserved its narrow streets and colourful, old-fashioned, charming façades. A city that has also been able to produce fashionable new addresses, *petiscos* (Portuguese tapas bars) and a youthful, trend-setting population. Lisbon swallowed me up whole for a delicious while, in a flurry of new people and food discoveries.

... TO THE HEART OF LISBON

Rua das Flores is the heart of the city for many Lisboetas. Taberna da rua das Flores (see page 295), a tavern in a small dark street, is lit up by the generous hearts of owner André and his team. In its cosy surroundings, I immediately felt the soul of a country, a passion for the produce... and my stomach felt it too! André, his young business partner Tiago and his team prepare traditional Portuguese dishes with just the right touch of a modern twist. The food is unassuming, light and fresh, joyful, intoxicating and so tantalizing, introducing me to the cooking of the city and luring me in.

There are no good recipes without great products and their talented producers. Thankfully, André knows lots of them and put me in touch with Rosa, his fishmonger. This charming lady and her colleagues work with incredible dexterity as they busily prepare the day's catch. Due to the language barrier, this was a meeting without words: though we had to make do by gesturing and smiling at each other, I barely required my translation app to let her know I absolutely needed her to tell me the story of her fishery. It was clear how vital she was to the city's food culture.

Another steer from André came after I tasted the unique bread on offer at his restaurant. I needed to find out how these extraordinarily dense, moist and smooth loaves were made. So I went to meet the bakers at Gleba (see page 295), a warm, steamy place – itself not unlike an oven – filled with the enchanting scents of yeast, of fermentation and of perfectly baked golden crusts.

And no journey to the heart of Portuguese food culture would be complete without a detour into its traditional skills in fish and seafood canning. So I found myself at Conserveira de Lisboa, a little shop with an almost vintage vibe, but which carries its expertise lightly.

This shop has been tucked away here, only a stone's throw from the main tourist areas of Lisbon, for more than 40 years. The company is run by Tiago, a man who has decided to promote the canning work of three traditional brands from his country: Minor, Tricana and Prato do Mar. I also met Rita, his assistant, who explained how the canning is done, how the fishing seasons are observed, how each little can is wrapped by hand and how customers' packets are carefully tied with colourful thread. This is a temple dedicated to tuna, mackerel fillets, whole sardines in local oil or little squid with chilli pepper. I had to resist the desire to carry everything away in my suitcase so that I could slip a little treasure into each copy of this book...

As we leave, Rita tells me about the shop owner's girlfriend, the beautiful Ingrid, who ran Kasutera, sadly since closed (see pages 283 and 295). Ingrid is a brilliant, almost self-taught pastry chef, whose style lies halfway between the reserved elegance of Japan and the charm of southern Europe. And I'm glad Rita tipped me off: Ingrid really wowed me with *kasutera*, her trademark Lusitano-Japanese sponge cakes. She told me the story of this simple cake, which the Portuguese had taken to Japan in the 16th century, then left behind in the Land of the Rising Sun. Fortunately, a man with a passion for food, culture and both countries brought this sweet, moist cake back to Lisbon a dozen years ago. And that was enough for Ingrid to decide to learn the unique way of making it and to share it with us. *Obrigado* and *arigato*!

Later, I met the wonderful Manuela Brandão (see page 127), a chef based in the city's most popular market: Mercado Da Ribeira (see page 296). Manuela is a meticulous perfectionist, with absolute mastery of the recipes she wanted to share with us. She reminds me of one of my favourite chefs, the multi-award-winning Anne-Sophie Pic: she's just as gentle, delicate and sensitive, equally determined and an incredible ambassador for her art and the cooking of her country. Manuela took us on a tour of her beautiful, colourful cuisine: I felt as though I'd discovered a jewel. Her recipes are accessible and that's what makes her so special: she possesses the rare ability to pass on her knowledge and culture in a very straightforward way.

THE LAND OF EGGS

Portuguese pastries contain a lot of eggs. To understand why, we need to go back a few hundred years. In the 15th century, egg whites were used to clarify wine and to starch the clothes of the court grandees... so what could be done with the yolks? Women developed ranges of pastries known as *conventual* (which means traditionally made in convents, as it was nuns who produced these sweet yellow-tinged cakes). This tradition has remained at the heart of Portuguese pastry-making. The list of little cakes we discovered is a long one, including *toucinho do céu* (see page 159), *castanhas de ovos* (see page 275), *broinhas de gema* and *ovos do paraíso*. But, of course, at the top of the list is the famous *pastéis de nata* (also called *pastel de nata;* see page 279). Also invented in a convent, in the 19th century, these little custard tarts – which can be eaten warm or cold and served with cinnamon and icing sugar – have made Portuguese sweet treats famous the world over. The top-secret recipes from the country's most famous bakeries will never be revealed, but I'll be sharing my favourite home-cooked version, to which our Portuguese friends gave their stamp of approval.

Now, when asked, 'Why this book? Are you Portuguese?' I'm tempted to answer, 'No, but almost!' with humility and a deep sense of respect for all the women and men who have agreed to share with us just a slice of their lives. I hope you have a delightful and delicious stroll through our recipes.

CONTENTS

RICARDO LUCIO

THE TRADITIONALIST

Ricardo Lucio is the first chef we are meeting on our Portuguese adventure.
He grew up in the area around Lisbon and has worked in some of the finest
Michelin-starred kitchens in both Portugal and France. In the pages that follow, he
gives us some wonderful recipes from his homeland. Rather than show us a snapshot
of the colourful contemporary cuisine that fills his working life, instead Ricardo takes
us on a culinary journey to the heart of his Lisboeta roots, with simple, family-style,
profoundly traditional recipes.

SARDINE AÇORDA

SERVES **4** • PREPARATION: **20 MINUTES** • COOKING: **15 MINUTES**

A simple Portuguese one-bowl meal. Açordas are traditional Portuguese soups made with stale bread. Ricardo has given us here a classic version, adding sardines for the touch of the sea that is the true taste of Portugal.

1   Heat the stock in a saucepan and season with salt and pepper to taste.

2   Bring the measured water and the vinegar to the boil in a separate wide saucepan, then reduce the heat to a simmer.

3   When the water mixture is simmering, drop in the eggs one at a time and poach for 3–4 minutes.

4   Using a slotted spoon, remove the poached eggs and place them on a plate lined with kitchen paper. Set aside.

5   Meanwhile, season the sardines with coarse sea salt directly into the gills.

6   Heat a frying pan with a little olive oil over a high heat and fry the sardines until golden brown on both sides.

7   Take 4 warmed bowls. In each, arrange first a slice of bread, then the herbs, then a drizzle of olive oil and finally the garlic. Pour in the hot stock and leave to soak for a few minutes.

8   Add a poached egg on top of each just before serving, with the sardines.

INGREDIENTS
2 litres (3½ pints) cod stock, or other fish stock • 1 litre (1¾ pints) water • 1 tablespoon white wine vinegar • 4 eggs • 8 sardines, gutted but unscaled • olive oil • 4 slices of stale sourdough bread (3–4 days old) • Handful of herb leaves (such as coriander, parsley or mint) • 1 sliced garlic clove • Coarse sea salt • Salt and freshly ground black pepper

SARDINES

You'll find sardines everywhere in Portugal – simple, tasty and fragrant – as the country's signature ingredient. They are also a sign of summer, because that is when the shoals swim closer to the coast, plump and succulent, delicious and much sought-after...

THE SCIENCE

The sardine is a species in the *Clupeidae* family, which also includes herring. Depending on the Portuguese region, the fish are known as *célan* or *célerin*, *royan*, *sarda*, or *sardinyola*. (Pilchards are also sardines, but are larger, older fish.) The name 'sardine' comes from Sardinia, where the fish was common in the waters around the island.

BUYING AND COOKING

- Always buy the freshest sardines; they should have a consistent colour.
- The fish should be firm yet supple.
- Take care about how you arrange them over the flame of a barbecue grill, distributing the heat evenly between each fish. A hinged fish grill frame is very useful.
- Choose a slow, constant heat to ensure perfectly grilled sardines. The skin should be just golden when served.

SARDINES IN NUMBERS

- The Portuguese are the biggest fish eaters in Europe, consuming 60kg (132lb) each year for every person!
- In June, the Portuguese consume one tonne of sardines every minute, mainly in Lisbon, where the popular festival season (choose from the festivals of Santo António, São João, São Pedro...) provides many an occasion for tables and sardine braziers to be brought out into the streets.
- In Portugal, sardine fishing is limited to 180 days a year and is prohibited at the weekend. Maximum catches for each fishing day have been introduced under a national quota, to help the fishery to become more sustainable.

CLAMS,
STRAIGHT FROM
THE BEACH

SERVES **4 AS A STARTER** • PREPARATION: **15 MINUTES** • COOKING: **15 MINUTES**

Clams, cockles and all the other little shellfish are easy to find on Portugal's beaches and Ricardo has childhood memories of digging for clams and taking them straight home. Quick pan-frying with a few drops of olive oil and a little garlic is all that's needed to bring out the flavours of these simple seaside treats...

1   Rinse the clams in cold water with salt to remove all the sand, changing the water several times. Discard any shells that are open and do not close after being sharply tapped on the side of a sink.

2   Heat a little olive oil in a large frying pan which has a lid, add the garlic and sauté for a few minutes until it colours slightly. Don't let it burn, or it will turn bitter.

3   Add the clams to the pan, cover and leave to cook over a medium heat for about 4 minutes, shaking the pan every now and then.

4   As soon as the clams start to open, remove the lid. Increase the heat and add the white wine and coriander, then the lemon juice. Leave to cook for a further 1–2 minutes, until the clams are cooked (discard any shells that do not open).

5   Serve immediately.

INGREDIENTS
500g (1lb 2oz) clams, cleaned • Olive oil • 1 garlic clove, chopped • 1 glass of white wine • A few chopped coriander leaves • Juice of 1 lemon • Salt

BACALHAU
À BRÁS

SERVES **4** • PREPARATION: **20 MINUTES** • COOKING: **40 MINUTES** • SOAKING: **24 HOURS**

This is one of the most popular dishes in Portugal and there must be more than a hundred recipes for it! Here, Ricardo has opted for a simple, light version, an everyday meal which works well with a baby leaf salad and a vinaigrette, ideally made with Port vinegar.

1   Desalinate the fish for 24 hours in a bowl of water placed in the bottom of the refrigerator, changing the water 2–3 times during the soaking.

2   Place the drained cod in a wide pan of cold water. Heat until simmering, then turn off the heat and leave the fish to poach in the residual heat for 20 minutes. Drain. Once cold, flake the cod, removing the skin and bones.

3   Peel the potatoes and cut into matchsticks. Heat the oil in a frying pan and fry the potatoes for 4–5 minutes, then remove with a slotted spoon and spread out on a tray lined with kitchen paper.

4   Fry the onions until golden in the same oil, then add the cod and cook over a low heat for 3–4 minutes.

5   Break the eggs into a bowl, add the parsley and lightly beat. Pour the eggs and potatoes into the cod pan.

6   Cook for 2–3 minutes until the eggs scramble, then serve immediately.

CHEF'S TIP
Traditionally, black olives are served on top of the scrambled egg and salt cod mixture. If you wish, scatter them over just before serving.

INGREDIENTS
200g (7oz) salt cod • 400g (14oz) Palha potatoes (available in Portuguese grocery shops, or use any floury variety) • 200ml (7fl oz/⅓ pint) mild olive oil • 2 onions, finely sliced • 5 eggs • A few parsley leaves, chopped

SPARE RIBS
WITH FRENCH TOAST

SERVES **4** • PREPARATION: **40 MINUTES** • COOKING: **30 MINUTES** • MARINATING: **1 HOUR**

EQUIPMENT: **BLENDER**

Ricardo wanted to share with us this recipe for Portuguese-style savoury French toast, with his perfectly cooked and delicious spare ribs. The toast is a simple mixture of stale bread soaked in milk, a few tomatoes and olive oil.

INGREDIENTS

FOR FOR THE PORK AND MARINADE
1.5kg (3lb 5oz) pork ribs
1 garlic clove, crushed
1 glass of olive oil, plus more for the toast
½ glass of white wine
1 tablespoon paprika
Salt and freshly ground black pepper

FOR THE FRENCH TOAST
4 slices of stale farmhouse bread (3–4 days old)
100ml (3½fl oz) milk
1 garlic clove, peeled and left whole
1 onion, sliced
Leaves from a few parsley sprigs, chopped
4 ripe tomatoes, chopped
½ glass of white wine

1 **Prepare the marinated pork:** place the meat in a large non-reactive dish with all the marinade ingredients, turning to coat the ribs in the flavours. Set aside in a cool place for 1 hour.

2 **Prepare the French toast:** in a bowl, soak the bread in the milk for 15 minutes, then drain.

3 Brown the whole garlic clove in a frying pan with a little olive oil, then remove from the pan.

4 Add the onion and parsley to the garlic pan and leave to brown. Add the drained bread and chopped tomatoes.

5 Season to taste with salt and pepper and pour in the white wine. Leave to cook over a low heat for 10 minutes, stirring regularly. Set aside.

6 Preheat the oven to 200°C (400°F), Gas Mark 6.

7 Place all the pork marinade ingredients, but not the pork itself, in a blender and blend until emulsified. Place the ribs in a roasting dish. Spread the marinade paste over and roast in the oven for 25 minutes.

8 Serve the French toast in one dish and the pork in another.

CHEF'S TIP
The white wine can be replaced by vegetable stock, if you prefer.

ALMOND CAKE

SERVES **4–6** • PREPARATION: **15 MINUTES** • COOKING: **20 MINUTES**

EQUIPMENT: **23CM (9IN) ROUND CAKE TIN**

This easy-to-make cake reminds Ricardo of tea parties at his grandmother's, along with a crowd of his cousins, after coming back from the beach or the park. Like many pastries in Portugal, the recipe contains lots of eggs. The almonds, which are as important here as the sugar, give the cake a comforting, aromatic touch.

1 Preheat the oven to 190°C (375°F), Gas Mark 5. Butter and flour a 23cm (9in) cake tin.

2 Mix the sugar and ground almonds in a large bowl, then add the whole eggs and the egg yolks.

3 Add the cinnamon and flour and mix all the ingredients together until smooth, trying not to incorporate too much air.

4 Pour the mixture into the prepared tin and cook for 20 minutes.

5 Leave to cool, then remove from the tin and enjoy, dusted with icing sugar if you like.

INGREDIENTS
small knob of butter, for the tin • 100g (3½oz) plain flour, plus more for the tin • 500g (1lb 2oz) caster sugar • 500g (1lb 2oz) ground almonds • 6 eggs • 6 egg yolks • 1 teaspoon ground cinnamon • icing sugar, to dust (optional)

SARDINHAS *

MENU

SARDINHAS
+
BATATA
COZIDA
(BOILED POTATOES)

14,5€

ALADAS

TOMATE

PÁSSARITO MON AMOUR

A PORTUGUESE WINE BAR IN PARIS

César De Souza is a darling, an adorable and unfailingly generous chef with a dining room in the heart of Paris's 11th *arrondissement*. He has opened a little grocery shop, too, that provides a little Portuguese sunshine in the French capital. Here, you'll find everything you need to enjoy the flavours of Portugal: preserves, organic wines, herbs and spices and a few well-chosen oils. His recipes combine Portuguese tradition with Parisian flair, delivering a colourful, very personal vision of his home country's food.

BAGAFINA

SERVES **4** • PREPARATION: **15 MINUTES** • COOKING: **5 MINUTES** • MARINATING: **2–3 HOURS**

This is the Parisian version of the more rustic Portuguese bifana. *These little sandwiches can be nibbled on anywhere, at any time.*

1   **Prepare the marinade:** combine all the ingredients for the marinade in a large non-reactive dish and place the escalopes in it. Leave to marinate for 2–3 hours.

2   **Now for the sandwiches:** brown the meat in a frying pan in a little olive oil with the chopped onion and garlic.

3   Cut the baguettes in half and open them up.

4   Generously slather the baguettes with mustard, add the lightly seasoned greens, then the escalopes. Add a little more mustard to taste, then serve.

INGREDIENTS

FOR THE MARINADE
1 garlic clove, crushed • ½ onion, sliced • 1 bay leaf • 500ml (18fl oz) dry white wine • 50ml (2fl oz) vegetable oil • Coarse sea salt

FOR THE SANDWICHES
6 pork escalopes • Olive oil • ½ onion, finely chopped • 1 garlic clove, crushed • 2 baguettes • Portuguese mustard, or English mustard • Mixed salad leaves, or baby spinach • Salt and freshly ground black pepper

SMOKED HADDOCK TARTARE TOASTS,
SMASHED AVOCADO, RED ONION PICKLE

SERVES **4** • PREPARATION: **20 MINUTES** • COOKING: **5 MINUTES** • PICKLING: **1½ HOURS**

This may not seem traditionally Portuguese, but César was keen to share the recipe with us, to bring modernity and colour to his selection of dishes.

INGREDIENTS
1 red onion
1 tablespoon red wine vinegar
1 tablespoon white wine vinegar
2 ripe avocados
1 tablespoon olive oil
1 dried *pili-pili* (bird eye) chilli, crushed, or ¼–½ teaspoon cayenne pepper, to taste
Juice of 1 lemon
Juice of 1 lime
250g (9oz) skinless smoked haddock fillet
Seeded sourdough rye bread, sliced
A few sprigs of dill or chives, chopped
Sea salt flakes
Salt

1   Thinly slice the red onion and place in a non-reactive bowl. Pour over both vinegars and add a little salt. Set aside for the onion to lightly pickle for at least 1½ hours.

2   Slice the avocados and place in a salad bowl with the olive oil, crushed dried chilli or cayenne and most of the lemon and lime juice (reserve a few drops). Season with sea salt flakes to taste. Crush the mixture between your fingers until it has a creamy texture.

3   Cut the haddock into fine strips.

4   Lightly toast the bread.

5   Spread the toasts with the mashed avocado. Add the haddock strips, slices of pickled red onion and finish off with a sprinkling of chopped dill or chives and the remaining drops of lemon and lime juice.

CHEF'S TIP

You can also add a few more sea salt flakes at the end; this will add even more crunch and zing to your toasts.

PARISIAN-STYLE
CALDO VERDE

SERVES **4** • PREPARATION: **15 MINUTES** • COOKING: **1 HOUR**

EQUIPMENT: **BLENDER**

Portugal's legendary green soup is traditionally made from a type of curly cabbage that is readily available in Portugal, though not elsewhere. Here, César offers a new twist with kale, which is similarly curly but has smaller leaves.

1   In a saucepan, bring the measured water to the boil with some salt, the garlic, white wine, bay leaf, olive oil and cured ham. Peel the potatoes. When the water comes to the boil, plunge the potatoes in whole and cook until they are tender.

2   Meanwhile, strip the leaves from the kale and discard the tough ribs. Cut the leaves into thin strips, place in a bowl and add the vinegar and enough cold water to cover. Leave to soak for 10 minutes, then massage the leaves vigorously to soften their fibres. Drain.

3   Remove the cured ham and bay leaf from the pan. Remove the pan from the heat and blend the soup, then return to the boil slowly. When the soup is simmering, add the cabbage strips in small handfuls, to prevent the pot from cooling too much. Simmer slowly for 30 minutes: the cabbage should be very tender. Taste and add salt and olive oil if necessary.

4   Meanwhile, cook the *chouriço* slices in a dry pan until golden brown.

5   Serve the soup piping hot, adding the slices of *chouriço* on top at the last minute.

INGREDIENTS
1 litre (1¾ pints) water • 2 garlic cloves, chopped • 150ml (5fl oz/¼ pint) dry white wine • 1 bay leaf • 100ml (3½fl oz) olive oil, plus more if needed • 50g (1¾oz) dry-cured ham • 500g (1lb 2oz) waxy potatoes • 300g (10½oz) bunch of kale • 200ml (7fl oz/⅓ pint) white wine vinegar • A few slices of Portuguese *chouriço* • Salt

PÁSSARITO'S BACALHAU!

SERVES **4** • PREPARATION: **30 MINUTES** • COOKING: **40 MINUTES** • SOAKING: **24 HOURS**

EQUIPMENT: **BLENDER**

It's impossible to imagine talking about the food of Portugal without mentioning the hundreds, if not thousands, of recipes based on the country's favourite ingredient: salt cod. César's version is particularly appealing, with its use of colourful peppers which bring a touch of acidity and freshness to a dish which is often very strongly flavoured. Its elegant style will have you dreaming of taking a stroll along the banks of the Douro river... Serve with salad, mangetout or other greens.

INGREDIENTS
600g (1lb 5oz) salt cod (preferably Norwegian)
250ml (9fl oz) dry white wine
250ml (9fl oz) milk
1 bay leaf
2 red peppers
300ml (10fl oz/½ pint) olive oil, plus more to fry the onion
4 garlic cloves
Pinch of paprika
Pinch of cayenne pepper
A few coriander sprigs, roughly chopped
1 onion, thinly sliced
4 eggs, lightly beaten
A few chives
1 lemon, plus lemon wedges (optional) to serve

1   Desalinate the cod for 24 hours in a bowl of water placed in the bottom of the refrigerator, changing the water 2–3 times during the soaking. Drain and set aside.

2   Preheat the oven to 220°C (425°F), Gas Mark 7.

3   Put the white wine, milk and bay leaf in a large saucepan half-filled with boiling water. Once boiling, plunge in the cod. After the liquid returns to the boil, leave the fish to cook for 10 minutes, then turn off the heat. Drain and set the cod aside.

4   Meanwhile, halve the peppers and roast them in the oven, laid out on a baking tray lined with foil, for around 30 minutes. When the skins are starting to blacken, remove them from the oven and run them under cold water. Remove and discard the seeds and put the flesh in a blender with 200ml (7fl oz/⅓ pint) of the olive oil, 2 of the garlic cloves, the paprika and cayenne. Blend until smooth. Add more oil if necessary, to form a smooth sauce, then set aside.

5   Flake the cod, removing the skin and bones. Mix it in a bowl with the rest of the olive oil and the coriander.

6   Sweat the onion and the 2 remaining garlic cloves, finely chopped, in a frying pan with a little oil. Add the flaked cod. When it starts to cook, add the eggs. Stir, then turn off the heat: the eggs should remain fairly runny.

7   Place the cod and eggs on a plate, then pour the pepper sauce on top. Add a few chives and a squeeze of lemon juice, then serve, with lemon wedges if you like.

A PORTUGUESE WINE BAR IN PARIS – **45**

SPICY TOMATO
TARTARE
WITH TUNA

SERVES **4** • PREPARATION: **20 MINUTES** • MARINATING: **1 HOUR**

EQUIPMENT: **4 × 8–10CM (3¼–4IN) RING MOULDS**

Bring sunshine to your table with this simple tomato salad with tuna. And not just any tuna: this is made using fish from Lisbon's traditional canners. César's favourite canned fish shops are Loja das Conservas and Conserveira de Lisboa (see page 297)... You won't need to look elsewhere; this pair of specialists have the best in the country.

INGREDIENTS
6 large ripe-but-firm tomatoes
2 tablespoons olive oil
2 tablespoons white wine vinegar
3 garlic cloves, finely chopped
1 red onion, finely chopped
1 teaspoon hot sauce with whisky, or chilli powder,
plus more to taste
Bunch of coriander, roughly chopped
Bunch of chives, roughly chopped
2 cans of best-quality tuna fillets in olive oil, drained
1 lemon
Sea salt flakes

1   Cut the tomatoes into quarters and remove and discard the seeds, chop the flesh finely, then put it into a sieve to drain away as much of the tomato liquid as possible.

2   Pour the olive oil and vinegar into a salad bowl. Add sea salt flakes to taste, then add the garlic and onion with the hot sauce or chilli powder. Mix and leave to marinate for at least 1 hour.

3   Season to taste, making sure the chilli heat is as you like it.

4   Just before serving, mix the chopped tomato with the marinade, coriander and most of the chives. Divide the mixture between 4 × 8–10cm (3¼–4in) ring moulds or tall pastry cutters, pressing down lightly to hold it together. Place a few pieces of canned tuna fillet on top of each.

5   Sprinkle with the reserved chives, add a squeeze of lemon juice and serve with dressed leaves of your choice.

CHEF'S TIP
For an even stronger flavour, open the can of tuna fillets ahead of time, place a couple of crushed garlic cloves on top and leave the oil to absorb the garlicky flavour for a good hour.

THE CANNERY

In 1938, there were 152 canneries across Portugal. Today, there are only about 20 left, but canned fish is still hugely popular across the country. The Portuguese consider seafood in cans a real delicacy and even include it on restaurant menus. They bring their own style to the store cupboard staple, with beautiful, imaginative packaging, so pretty that you can't decide whether to display it or eat it!

HOW TO CAN FISH THE TRADITIONAL PORTUGUESE WAY

1. Season the fish with salt.
2. Pre-cook it by steaming: this will allow the fish to lose some of its fat but keep a powerful flavour.
3. Put the fish in a can with other flavouring ingredients, such as dried *piri-piri* (bird eye) chilli or herbs.
4. Fill the cans with a heated liquid, usually oil such as olive or sunflower, or a sauce such as tomato.
5. Seal the cans and sterilize them. This step provides a second cooking process and enables the good long keeping period.

THE CONSERVEIRA DE LISBOA

This company (see page 297) has been trading in the Baixa district of Lisbon since 1930, back then under the name Mercearia do Minho, and has remained in the same family since it opened. The Conserveira has always maintained the same principle: providing a traditionally manufactured and high-quality product to its customers. The shop décor has not changed and thousands of cans are piled on the shelves, right up to the ceiling. The preserves are, of course, based on sardines, but there is also tuna, octopus, cod, mussels and other shellfish.

All the fish is sourced in Portugal, with the exception of salmon and cod. The two main seasonal fish are sardines and tuna, both in season during summer. Exports represent around 10 per cent of the Conserveira's canning business, with France and Italy the top destinations for these colourful cans.

'NUN'S BOTTOM' SALAD

SERVES **4** • PREPARATION: **15 MINUTES** • COOKING: **30 MINUTES** • SOAKING: **1 HOUR** • MARINATING: **1 HOUR**

What a strange name! Don't worry, no nuns are harmed in the making of this salad. It is just the nickname César gives to these slightly sweet beans, more regularly known as black-eyed peas. This easy-to-make delightful salad has fresh, spicy notes and is perfect for any occasion. Not unlike Black Eyed Peas, the famous pop group of the 2000s...

INGREDIENTS

FOR THE SALAD
250g (9oz) dried black-eyed peas (from Portuguese or Asian grocery shops)
1 bay leaf
1 garlic clove, crushed
100g (3½oz) *requeijão de cabra* (fresh Portuguese goat's cheese), or other good-quality fresh goat's cheese (optional)

FOR THE TOMATO CONFIT MARINADE
5 tablespoons olive oil
1 tablespoon white wine vinegar
Bunch of flat-leaf parsley, leaves roughly chopped
3 garlic cloves, finely chopped
Bunch of spring onions, or 1 red onion, finely sliced
Pinch of sweet paprika, or cumin seeds
100g (3½oz) sun-dried tomatoes in oil, finely chopped
Sea salt flakes

1. **For the salad:** soak the black-eyed peas in a bowl of cold water for at least 1 hour.

2. Put a large pan of salted water on to boil with the bay leaf and crushed garlic clove. Add the drained soaked black-eyed peas to the boiling water and leave to cook for 20–30 minutes over a high heat. They should still be al dente.

3. **Meanwhile, prepare your tomato confit marinade:** in a salad bowl, mix the olive oil and white wine vinegar with a pinch of sea salt flakes. Add the parsley, garlic, spring onions or red onion and paprika or cumin seeds. Add the sun-dried tomatoes, then add them to the marinade.

4. Mix the still-warm black-eyed peas with the marinade and set aside in the refrigerator for 1 hour.

5. Serve with a little *requeijão de cabra* cheese on top, if you like.

OCTOPUS SALAD
FROM THE BEIRAS

SERVES **4** • PREPARATION: **30 MINUTES** • COOKING: **40 MINUTES** • MARINATING: **1 HOUR**

The Beiras are three regions of Portugal, between the Atlantic coast and the mountains. All the flavours of the country can be found here: from the picturesque seaside resorts and villages, to the beautiful vineyards and flourishing agriculture. Octopus is one of the basic ingredients of everyday cooking, as the catch is very good on the Portuguese coast.

1   **For the octopus:** heat a pan of salted water and add the red onion, white wine and bay leaf. When it comes to the boil, plunge in the octopus, then reduce the heat so that the water is hot, but never boils. Cook for 20–30 minutes, depending on the size of the tentacles (those of the biggest octopuses will need up to 40 minutes).

2   **Meanwhile, prepare the marinade:** put all the ingredients in a bowl and stir well to combine.

3   After cooking, rinse the octopus in cold water, carefully wash and clean the tentacles and thoroughly remove the skin. Cut the thicker parts into fairly thin sections, leaving the thinner parts in longer lengths, then add to the bowl of marinade and leave to marinate for at least 1 hour.

4   Serve with mixed salad leaves, maybe with crusty bread, or steamed baby potatoes drizzled with olive oil.

INGREDIENTS

FOR THE OCTOPUS
½ red onion, peeled • 150ml (5fl oz/¼ pint) dry white wine • 1 bay leaf • 1kg (2lb 4oz) fresh giant octopus tentacles • Mixed leaves, to serve

FOR THE MARINADE
1 red or yellow pepper, thinly sliced • 1 red onion, thinly sliced • 2–4 garlic cloves, to taste, finely chopped • A few sprigs of coriander, chopped • A few sprigs of chives, finely chopped • Juice of ½ lemon • Juice of ½ lime • 3 tablespoons olive oil • 1 tablespoon white wine vinegar • Sea salt flakes

GRILLED SCALLOPS
AND SALPICÃO

SERVES **4 AS A STARTER** • PREPARATION: **15 MINUTES** • COOKING: **5 MINUTES** •
MARINATING: **1 HOUR**

Salpicão is a typical Portuguese sausage. Formed only of lean meat (traditionally always pork), thigh, shoulder and fillet, this dried, fermented sausage is cut into large pieces and marinated for a fortnight in red wine and spices, before being very delicately cold smoked. Find it at a Portuguese grocery shop, or online.

1   Marinate the scallops for 1 hour in a non-reactive bowl with the mixed hot sauces, or hot sauce and chilli powder, and a little olive oil. Meanwhile, brown the slices of *salpicão* in a dry frying pan.

2   Heat a clean frying pan until very hot, then fry the marinated scallops for 2–3 minutes on each side. You won't need to add oil, as there is oil in the marinade. Add the whisky, stand back, then light the alcohol with a long-handled match, or by tipping the pan towards the flame.

3   Arrange the *salpicão* slices in a rosette on warmed plates, sprinkle with sea salt flakes and then add the scallops on top, with any sauce from the pan.

4   Scatter with chopped chives and serve immediately.

CHEF'S TIP
For extra flavour, deglaze the pan with balsamic vinegar before pouring the sauce over the scallops.

INGREDIENTS
12 fresh scallops • 1 teaspoon *piri-piri* (bird eye) chilli sauce • 1 teaspoon hot sauce with whisky, or chilli powder • Olive oil • About 20 slices of *salpicão* • 1 shot of whisky • A few chives, finely chopped • Sea salt flakes

CHOCOLATE ORANGE CLOUD

SERVES **4** • PREPARATION: **10 MINUTES** • COOKING: **10 MINUTES** • CHILLING: **1–2 HOURS**

EQUIPMENT: **WHIPPING SIPHON**

Every Portuguese restaurant has its own version of chocolate mousse and Pássarito's recipe is light and tangy. Siphons at the ready!

1   Bring the milk and cream to the boil in a saucepan. Put the chocolate in a heatproof bowl.

2   Once it is boiling, pour the milk–cream mixture over the chocolate and stir to a smooth consistency.

3   Stir in the Grand Marnier®. Pour the mixture into a whipping siphon, close and chill for 1–2 hours.

4   Meanwhile, remove the zest and pith from the orange and segment the fruit, then chop the segments into small pieces. Once the chocolate cream is well chilled, add 2 cartridges of gas to the siphon.

5   Half-fill 4 stemmed glasses with siphoned chocolate mousse, then add a layer of small pieces of orange and sprinkle over most of the *speculoos*. Finish filling the glass with siphoned mousse and sprinkle with the remaining *speculoos*. Serve immediately.

CHEF'S TIP
Replace the Grand Marnier® with lavender, if you like, infused into the cream as it is heated up.

INGREDIENTS
250ml (9fl oz) whole milk • 250ml (9fl oz) whipping cream (30 per cent fat) • 125g (4½oz) plain chocolate, finely chopped • 1 tablespoon Grand Marnier® (or see chef's tip, above) • 1 orange • 2–3 *speculoos* biscuits, crumbled

PÁSSARITO'S
TORTA DE LARANJA

SERVES **6–8** • PREPARATION: **30 MINUTES** • COOKING: **40 MINUTES** •
STANDING: **30 MINUTES**

EQUIPMENT: **KITCHEN BLOWTORCH**

To finish off this gourmet tour with César, here is a traditional orange roll... with lots of eggs, of course, the starting point of all Portuguese desserts!

INGREDIENTS

FOR THE CAKE
Butter, for the tray
2 unwaxed oranges
50g (1¾oz) plain flour
8 eggs
200g (7oz) brown sugar
50g (1¾oz) caster sugar, plus more to sprinkle

FOR THE ORANGE CRÈME PÂTISSIÈRE
2 eggs, separated
50g (1¾oz) brown sugar
50g (1¾oz) plain flour, sifted
250ml (9fl oz) whole milk

FOR THE CINNAMON MERINGUE
1 tablespoon icing sugar
1 tablespoon ground cinnamon

1. Preheat the oven to 200°C (400°F), Gas Mark 6. Butter a rectangular baking tray, about 33 × 22cm (13 × 8½in), line it with baking parchment, then butter the paper too.

2. **Start with the cake:** rinse the oranges. Finely grate the zest and set aside, then juice the fruit.

3. Sift the flour into a bowl and mix with the orange juice, whisking until smooth and making sure no lumps form. In a separate bowl, beat the 8 eggs with the 200g (7oz) brown sugar. Once the mixture is smooth, stir in the flour-juice mixture. Pour this mixture into the prepared baking tray and bake for 30 minutes.

4. **Meanwhile, prepare the orange *crème pâtissière*:** beat the 2 egg yolks in a bowl (reserve the whites). Add the sugar to the yolks, mix, then fold in the sifted flour. Gradually stir in 100ml (3½fl oz) of the milk, keeping the mixture smooth and trying not to incorporate too much air. Heat the rest of the milk in a small saucepan. When it starts to bubble, but not boil, add the flour mixture and the reserved orange zest. Stir until the mixture thickens, then remove from the heat.

5. **For the meringue:** in a clean bowl, whisk the egg whites, icing sugar and ground cinnamon until smooth and glossy. Set aside in a cool place.

6. Turn the still-warm cake out on to a clean tea towel sprinkled with sugar. Spread the orange *crème pâtissière* over the cake, then gently roll it up. Leave the cake to cool to room temperature.

7. Once the cake has cooled, top with the cinnamon meringue using a piping bag or a spatula. Use a kitchen blowtorch to lightly brown the meringue, then serve immediately.

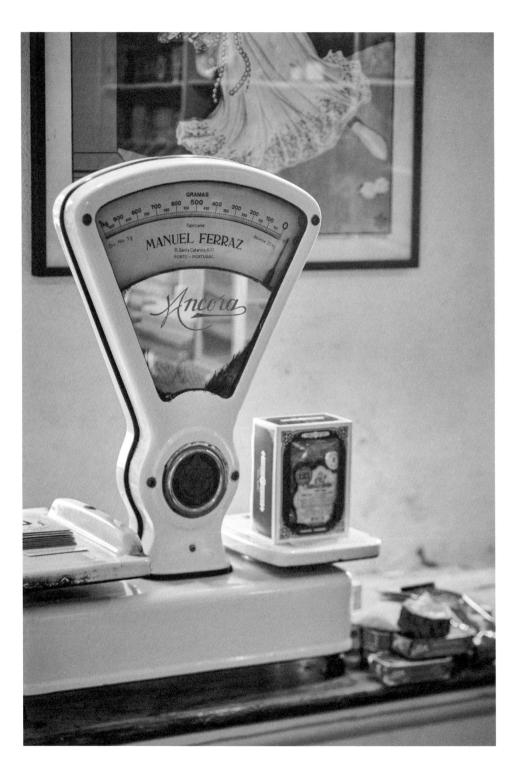

LES COMPTOIRS DE LISBONNE

BISTRO FOOD

Les Comptoirs de Lisbonne (see page 295) is the creation of a fun and sparkling couple: Malika Boudiba in the dining room, Fernando Martins behind the bar. When Fernando realized he was homesick for Portugal, he decided to transform his Parisian restaurant into a charming neighbourhood Portuguese-style eatery, complete with colour, life, local regulars and a good dose of spice and flavour. Here are a few of the pair's favourite and delicious recipes.

FLAMBÉED CHOURIÇO

SERVES **4 AS A STARTER** • PREPARATION: **20 MINUTES** • COOKING: **5 MINUTES**

EQUIPMENT: **TERRACOTTA FLAMBÉ DISH (OPTIONAL)**

An assador de chouriço or chorizo grill is a typically Portuguese glazed earthenware dish used to flambé chouriços and other Portuguese smoked sausages. You can use any favourite ovenproof and flameproof dish which you would also use for serving.

1   Preheat the oven to 200°C (400°F), Gas Mark 6.

2   Slice into the *chouriço* two-thirds of the way through at 1–2cm (½–¾ in) intervals, being sure not to separate the sausage into pieces.

3   Place the *chouriço* in an earthenware flambé dish, or ovenproof and flameproof dish (see recipe introduction) and bake on a high shelf in the oven for 10 minutes.

4   Remove from the oven, place on a flameproof surface and carefully pour over the *aguardente*, being sure not to spill it. If any is spilled out of the dish, you will have to clean it up immediately, as that can be a fire risk.

5   Carefully flambé the *chouriço* in the alcohol with a long-handled match.

6   Turn the *chouriço* over with a knife after 2–3 minutes of flambéing, then extinguish the flames. Enjoy!

CHEF'S TIP
Portuguese aguardente is a strong spirit with a high alcohol content that is either distilled from wine or made from fruit and grains. The word literally means 'fire water'.

INGREDIENTS
1 Portuguese *chouriço,* weighing about 200g (7oz) • 150ml (5fl oz/¼ pint) *aguardente* (see chef's tip, above)

CHARCUTERIE

There is a marvellous variety of Portuguese charcuterie, with more than 70 types of cured and smoked sausage and other cured meats.

THE PORTUGUESE ART OF SMOKING

Traditional Portuguese charcuterie is the product of the ancient national art of smoking, as well as of the country's distinctive, rugged and relatively lean pigs. Both these have given the country's cured meats the inimitable characteristics that make its flavours unique.

OUR FAVOURITES

- **Cacholeira branca de Portalegre PGI:** a sausage from the Alto Alentejo region, which looks like a black pudding. Since 1997, it has held the European Union's Protected Geographical Indication (PGI) status. It is often cooked before eating.

- **Chouriço de carne:** this is the leanest *chouriço* in its category. It is used in classic *caldo verde* (see page 259), where it adds its hint of spice and smoky notes.

- **Chouriço corrente:** the fattiest *chouriço*! It is usually flambéed with brandy, and you must prick it all the way along before cooking, so that the fat runs out.

- **Chouriço de sangue, or morcela:** a kind of black pudding sometimes flavoured with with cumin and cloves.

- **Farinheira:** a smoked white pudding made from wheat flour and pork fat. It has a yellowish brown colour and appears in traditional dishes such as *feijoada* or *cozido a Portuguesa* (Portuguese stew). It can also be flambéed in brandy. Although it looks like a *chouriço*, it has a heavier texture.

- **Paio do lombo:** this is made from pork loin and is very delicate.

- *Linguiça de Portalegre:* another PGI product. Its characteristic flavour comes mainly from the use of meat and fat from pure-bred Alentejo pigs, which are fed a diet rich in acorns.

- **Paio York:** a traditional cured pork loin sausage, common to both Portugal and Brazil.

SALT COD FRITTERS

MAKES **12–15** • PREPARATION: **45 MINUTES** • COOKING: **45 MINUTES** • SOAKING: **24 HOURS**

EQUIPMENT: **DEEP FRYER** • **PROBE THERMOMETER (BOTH OPTIONAL)**

There are many variations of this dish: with or without onion, garlic or nutmeg... All of them, though, include potatoes and salt cod. This is simple and a delight for the taste buds!

1   Desalinate the cod for 24 hours in a bowl of water placed in the bottom of the refrigerator, changing the water 2–3 times during the soaking. Drain off the soaking water.

2   Place the cod in a wide saucepan of fresh cold water. Heat until the water is simmering, then turn off the heat and leave the cod to poach in the residual heat for 20 minutes. Drain. Once cold, flake the cod, removing the skin and bones. Set aside.

3   Cook the potatoes in salted water, or steam them for 25 minutes, then remove the skins. Mash to a purée.

4   Mix the flaked cod and mashed potatoes in a large bowl. Add the onions, parsley, nutmeg and salt and pepper to taste. Lightly beat the eggs in a separate bowl, add to the cod and mix until they bind the mixture well. Using 2 tablespoons, shape the mixture into fritters.

5   Heat the vegetable oil to 180°C (350°F), or until a piece of mixture, when thrown in, sizzles immediately. Carefully fry the fritters in batches, being careful not to overcrowd the pan. Once they are golden brown, take them out and drain them on a plate lined with kitchen paper. Serve with Portuguese *piri-piri* sauce.

INGREDIENTS

500g (1lb 2oz) salt cod fillets • 500g (1lb 2oz) potatoes, scrubbed but unpeeled • 2 onions, finely chopped • Bunch of parsley, leaves chopped • 1 teaspoon grated nutmeg • 5 eggs • Vegetable oil, to deep-fry • Salt and freshly ground black pepper • Portuguese *piri-piri* (bird eye) chilli sauce, to serve

PORTUGUESE SEAFOOD RICE

SERVES **4** • PREPARATION: **45 MINUTES** • COOKING: **30–40 MINUTES**

Portuguese-style seafood rice is a traditional dish found mainly by the sea, a lovely little stew made with fresh shellfish and local rice. It's easy to feel like you're on holiday with this recipe: away you go!

1   Rinse the clams in cold water with salt to remove all the sand, changing the water several times. Scrape and rinse the mussels. Discard any clams or mussels that are open. Rinse the prawns and crab claws.

2   Place the fish stock cubes in a saucepan with the measured boiling water.

3   Cut a cross in the skin at the base of each tomato, place in a heatproof bowl and pour over boiling water to cover. After 30 seconds, drain: the skins should slip off. Quarter the skinned tomatoes and remove the seeds.

4   In a saucepan, heat the olive oil and sauté the onions, garlic, bay leaves and tomatoes. Leave to simmer for 5 minutes over a medium heat.

5   Add the rice to the pan and stir for 3–4 minutes, then add the white wine and stir again for 3–4 minutes. Add the passata and a few ladles of the stock. Stir and simmer for 5 minutes, still over a medium heat. When the liquid has evaporated, add the seafood and a little more stock. Leave to cook, continuing to stir. Add stock as required, as the rice needs to be very moist, like a risotto. Discard any clams or mussels that have not opened. Season with salt and pepper.

6   Arrange the rice in 4 large warmed bowls, distributing the seafood evenly, add the coriander and serve!

INGREDIENTS
400g (14oz) clams • 400g (14oz) mussels • 400g (14oz) prawns • 4 crab claws • 2 fish stock cubes • 1.5 litres (3¼ pints) boiling water • 4 tomatoes • 4 tablespoons olive oil • 2 onions, chopped • 3 garlic cloves, chopped • 2 bay leaves • 400g (14oz) white *Carolino* rice • 100ml (3½fl oz) white wine • 400g (14oz) tomato passata • Bunch of coriander, chopped • Salt and freshly ground black pepper

PORK STEW
WITH CLAMS

SERVES **4** • PREPARATION: **1 HOUR 10 MINUTES** • COOKING: **40 MINUTES** •
MARINATING: **AT LEAST 6 HOURS**

A very traditional Portuguese stew made with pork and clams, which is a typical (and delicious) combination in this country. The sauce is easy to make.

INGREDIENTS

FOR THE PORK
300ml (10fl oz/½ pint) dry white wine
1 teaspoon paprika
2½ teaspoons salt
¼ teaspoon freshly ground black pepper
2 garlic cloves
1 bay leaf
600g (1lb 5oz) pork fillet, chopped into bite-sized chunks
1 teaspoon olive oil

FOR THE CLAMS
2 teaspoons olive oil
2 onions, sliced into very thin rings
3 garlic cloves, crushed
2 tomatoes, skinned (see page 83) and finely chopped
¼ teaspoon chilli powder
20 small clams, well-scrubbed
Handful of chopped parsley leaves

1 **Prepare the marinated pork:** mix the wine, paprika, salt and pepper in a bowl. Cut the 2 garlic cloves in half and add them to the mixture with the bay leaf, then add the pork and mix to coat the chunks of meat in the marinade.

2 Leave to rest in a cool place for at least 6 hours, turning the meat over from time to time.

3 Remove the meat from the marinade and pat dry. Keep the marinade aside, discarding the garlic and bay leaf.

4 Brown the pork over a high heat with the 1 teaspoon of oil, stirring regularly. Remove the meat from the pan and set aside in a bowl.

5 Pour the rest of the marinade into the pan and bring to the boil, scraping the base of the pan a little to release the cooking juices. Leave to boil uncovered until the marinade has reduced by one-third. Pour this sauce over the pork and set aside.

6 **Now for the clams:** heat the oil in a casserole pan over a medium heat and soften the onions for 5 minutes, stirring, until they are tender (they should not brown).

7 Add the garlic, tomatoes and chilli. Leave to simmer for 5 minutes, stirring from time to time.

8 Meanwhile, rinse the clams in cold water with salt to remove all the sand, changing the water several times. Discard any clams that are open, then arrange the rest in a single layer in the tomato sauce. Cover the pan and cook over a medium heat for 10 minutes, until all the clams are open. Discard any that have not opened.

9 Add the pork and its sauce to the clam pan, then leave to simmer for 5 minutes. Serve in warmed soup plates, sprinkled with the parsley.

FEIJOADA-STYLE
GRILLED
RIB-EYE STEAK

SERVES **4** • PREPARATION: **30 MINUTES** • COOKING: **1¾ HOURS** • SOAKING: **2 HOURS** •
MARINATING: **30 MINUTES**

Feijoada is a typical Brazilian-Portuguese stew, which is usually pork or beef simmered with bacon, onion and black beans. There's no slow-cooked meat in this recipe, just excellent marinated steak served with a spicy sauce and feijoada-style black beans. Simpler, quicker and just as delicious!

INGREDIENTS
500g (1lb 2oz) dried black beans
1 bay leaf
Olive oil
100g (3½oz) smoked bacon lardons
1 onion, chopped
2 garlic cloves, chopped
1 teaspoon black peppercorns
1 tablespoon chilli paste
1kg (2lb 4oz) rib-eye steak
100ml (3½fl oz) white wine
Sea salt flakes
Freshly ground black pepper

1   Soak the beans in a bowl with plenty of cold water for 2 hours, then drain
    them and put them in a saucepan with the bay leaf. Just-cover with water.
    Bring to the boil and cook for 45 minutes, until tender, topping up with
    water if the pan is running dry, but only just covering the beans if you do.
    If you didn't have time to soak the beans, extend the cooking time by
    15–30 minutes. Turn off the heat and leave the beans in their cooking
    liquid. Set aside.

2   Heat a drizzle of oil in a large, deep frying pan and put in the lardons and
    onion. Once they are golden brown, pour in the black beans along with
    their cooking liquid. Bring to the boil and boil for 30 minutes to thicken
    the liquid. If at the end of this time the sauce is still too runny (check the
    photo on the previous page for the desired consistency), then strain the
    pan over a bowl, return the liquid to the pan and reduce it further, before
    returning the beans. Check the seasoning and adjust if necessary.

3   Put the garlic in a mortar with the black peppercorns, a pinch of sea salt
    flakes and the chilli paste. Mash all the ingredients to a smooth paste.

4   Spread the paste over the rib-eye steak, then place the meat on a large
    ovenproof tray. Drizzle with the white wine and a little more olive oil and
    leave to sit for 30 minutes.

5   Preheat the oven to 220°C (425°F), Gas Mark 7.

6   Cook the steak in the oven for 15 minutes, turning it occasionally and
    basting it with the sauce in the tray, until the meat is golden brown. It
    should still be rare in the centre. Leave to rest for 5 minutes.

7   Serve the sliced meat topped with the rest of the sauce, accompanied by
    the black beans and a bowl of white rice.

CHEF'S TIP
*If necessary, add a little water to the sauce to prevent the meat from
drying out.*

TABERNA DA RUA DAS FLORES

A TOP-NOTCH TABERNA

It was the lilting name of this little tavern that I kept coming back to, in my quest to find the best of Portuguese cuisine. Our arrival at Taberna da Rua das Flores (see page 295) was exactly as we had imagined. A little alley. No flashy lighting. No glaring sign. Just a door left ajar into André Magalhães's down-to-earth world. André's tavern is an ode to his diners and the pleasure of entertaining. Historically, taverns were located in these little neighbourhood houses, where the men would come by to collect coal and wine on their return from work. Little by little, the tavern became a charming, sociable place where tasty, comforting dishes were prepared. That is the kind of tavern that André has preserved, while adding a fresh, contemporary twist.

SALT COD AND CHICKPEA SALAD

SERVES **4** • PREPARATION: **30 MINUTES** • COOKING: **25 MINUTES** • SOAKING: **24 HOURS**

La meia desfeita de bacalhau *is a typical dish from the Mouraria district of Lisbon, mentioned as far back as the late 19th century by writers such as Eça de Queirós and Ramalho Ortigão in the monthly publication* As Farpas. *This popular recipe used the more economical tails and offcuts of the fish, for those who couldn't afford the prime pieces of cod. At Taberna da Rua das Flores, they have rebooted this ancestral recipe using chickpeas, salt cod, eggs and hot chilli powder.*

1   Desalinate the cod for 24 hours in a bowl of water placed in the bottom of the refrigerator, changing the water 2–3 times during the soaking. Drain off the soaking water.

2   Place the cod in a wide saucepan of fresh cold water. Heat until the water is simmering, then turn off the heat and leave the cod to poach in the residual heat for 20 minutes. Drain. Once cold, flake the fish, removing the skin and bones.

3   Mix together the onion and garlic, parsley and 1 grated hard-boiled egg. Place half of this mixture in a large bowl and add the chickpeas. Mix well. Season with the olive oil, vinegar, pepper and a pinch of sea salt flakes.

4   Arrange on a serving dish. Place the flaked cod on top, scatter with the rest of the red onion mixture and the remaining 4 hard-boiled eggs, quartered. Sprinkle with hot chilli powder to taste and finish off with a final drizzle of olive oil to serve.

INGREDIENTS
500g (1lb 2oz) salt cod • 1 red onion, finely chopped • 4 garlic cloves, finely chopped • leaves from 1 sprig of parsley, finely chopped • 5 hard-boiled eggs • 500g (1lb 2oz) cooked chickpeas, drained • 3 tablespoons extra virgin olive oil, plus more to serve • 1 tablespoon red wine vinegar • Hot chilli powder • Freshly ground white pepper • Sea salt flakes

FISH

Our friend André Magalhães from Taberna da Rua das Flores told us all about Rosa. He said she was the best fishmonger in Lisbon and invited us to visit her very early one morning at Rosanamar at the Mercado da Ribeira (see page 295). We didn't hesitate for a second, and discovered the wonders of the sea that Rosa works with so passionately alongside her all-female team. Beautiful, concentrated faces, the desire to excel, the pleasure of working with the richest resources the sea has to offer: that's Rosa's way. In fact, her slogan is '*O mar dà, a Rosa entrega...*', which means, 'What the sea gives, Rosa delivers'.

PORTUGAL'S BOUNTY

Rosa supplies fish to some of the finest dining locations in the city, including top chefs such as José Avillez at his food hall (see page 296), as well as to my favourite Lisboeta restaurants, such as the Taberna da Rua das Flores (see page 97).

Portugal is a country steeped in marine influences, with a coastline out of proportion to its land mass, rich in shellfish, molluscs and a wide variety of fish.

- **To the north**: trout rivers.
- **In the centre**: sea bream, which is in season during November and December (on the Setúbal coast).
- **To the south:** the most commonly caught fish are sea bass (robalo), gilthead bream, common bream and sargo bream (dourada, pargo and sargo), red mullet (salmonete) and, of course, sardines (sardinhas), which are available from June until the end of September.

ROSA AND HER PASSION FOR FISH

Rosa works with tuna, sardines, octopus and small fish caught just off the coast near Lisbon, including eels, red mullet, sargo bream (a typically Portuguese fish), prawns and clams. All these treasures take centre stage on the top restaurant tables of the capital, just a few hours after they leave her skilled hands. There is a natural feeling for the sea and its bounty in Lisbon, which all the chefs and restaurants of the city are continually celebrating and reinventing.

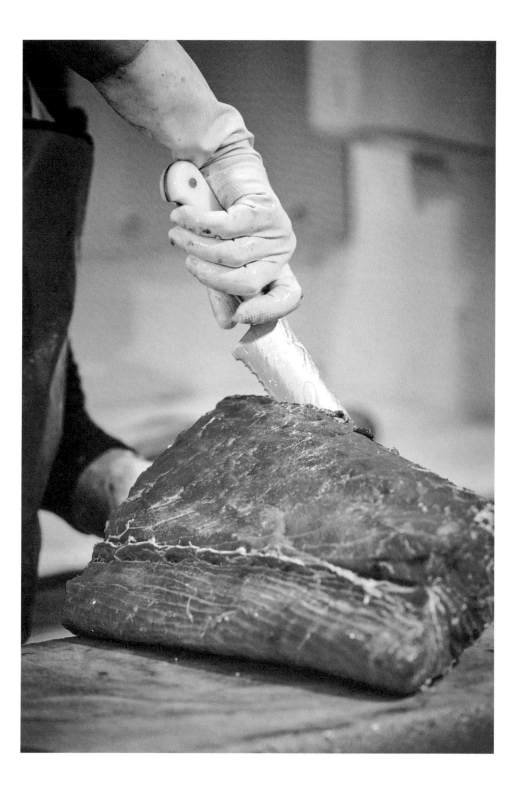

OCTOPUS
WITH SWEET POTATO

SERVES **4** • PREPARATION: **30 MINUTES** • COOKING: **1 HOUR**

EQUIPMENT: **PRESSURE COOKER**

Here's our old friend the octopus: vibrant, fresh, almost sparkling. Combined with the freshness of thyme and coriander, the spiciness of the pepper and the paprika, it is truly at its best. This dish is an absolute must.

1   Place the octopus tentacles in a large bowl and massage vigorously with the coarse salt for 5 minutes. Rinse in cold water, then drain.

2   Place the octopus in a pressure cooker with the bouquet garni and only just enough water to cover. Close the pressure cooker, bring to medium pressure, then cook for 15 minutes. Depressurize the cooker, then drain the octopus and set aside.

3   Meanwhile, preheat the oven to 200°C (400°F), Gas Mark 6.

4   Wash the sweet potatoes, give them a good scrub, then cut them into thick slices and place in an ovenproof dish (in Portugal they would use stoneware) with half the olive oil, half the garlic cloves, the chopped thyme, most of the coriander (reserve a little) and some ground black pepper. Bake for 40 minutes, stirring occasionally.

5   Heat a small frying pan with the remaining olive oil and garlic. When the garlic is golden, add the vinegar, more ground pepper and the paprika.

6   Cut the tentacles into sections and arrange on warmed plates with the sweet potatoes. Drizzle with the garlic and vinegar sauce and scatter with a few chopped coriander leaves to serve.

INGREDIENTS
1kg (2lb 4oz) octopus tentacles • 1kg (2lb 4oz) coarse sea salt • 1 bouquet garni • 1kg (2lb 4oz) sweet potatoes • 100ml (3½fl oz) olive oil • 12 garlic cloves, crushed • Leaves from 1 sprig of thyme, chopped • Small bunch of coriander, chopped • 2 tablespoons white wine vinegar • Paprika • Freshly ground black pepper

HORSE MACKEREL TARTARE

SERVES **4 AS A STARTER** • PREPARATION: **20 MINUTES** • SOAKING: **30 MINUTES** •
CHILLING: **10 MINUTES**

EQUIPMENT: **4 × 8–10CM (3¼–4IN) RING MOULDS**

Picadinho de carapau. *A tasty, simple and economical recipe always featured on the taverna's menu, this is a testament to the owner's commitment to food that is accessible to all. Brought a bit up to date with tangy notes, horse mackerel tartare is an essential dish.*

INGREDIENTS
600g (1lb 5oz) skinless boneless horse mackerel fillets
1 unwaxed orange
1 unwaxed lemon
1 unwaxed lime
50g (1¾oz) dried wakame seaweed
2 tablespoons extra virgin olive oil, plus more to serve
80g (2¾oz) green apple (about ½)
80g (2¾oz) red pepper (about ½), finely chopped
80g (2¾oz) yellow pepper (about ½), finely chopped
1 small red onion, finely chopped
80g (2¾oz) celery stalks (1–2), finely chopped
2 tablespoons chopped coriander leaves
2 tablespoons soy sauce
2 tablespoons finely chopped peeled root ginger
1 tablespoon sesame oil
1 tablespoon toasted black and white sesame seeds
½ tablespoon dried shrimps
Sea salt flakes

1   Cut the horse mackerel fillets into 1cm (½in) cubes and set aside in a cool place.

2   Finely grate the zest from the citrus fruit with a zester and set aside in a small glass bowl with the juice of the fruits.

3   Put the seaweed in a small bowl of cold water to soak for 30 minutes. Drain, cut it into strips, then return to the empty bowl and add half the citrus fruit juice and zest and 1 tablespoon of the olive oil.

4   Finely chop the apple and place in a chilled glass bowl. Mix in the horse mackerel, peppers, onion, celery and coriander leaves. Add the soy sauce, ginger, sesame oil, remaining 1 tablespoon of olive oil, a pinch of salt and the remaining zest and juice of the citrus fruits. Refrigerate for 10 minutes.

5   Place a bed of seaweed in the centre of each plate and arrange the tartare on top using a ring mould. Sprinkle with a few sesame seeds and the dried shrimps. Season it all with a drizzle of olive oil and sea salt flakes and serve the tartares immediately.

OYSTER TARTARE

MAKES **4** • PREPARATION: **30 MINUTES** • MARINATING: **30 MINUTES**

Portuguese oysters: fleshy, a good size, just the right touch of iodine… Here, they are prepared with several Japanese-inspired condiments, creating a beautifully fresh, powerful tartare. The bitter seaweed and the acidity of the lemon pack a real punch. This recipe is an ideal: just use whatever fresh green seaweed you are able to buy.

1 Open the oysters. Collect the liquor and store it in a glass bowl in a cool place.

2 Remove the meat from the oysters and marinate in a non-reactive bowl in the buttermilk for 30 minutes, then drain. Set the shells aside to serve in.

3 Finely chop all the sea greens. Set aside a few of the more attractive leaves and sprigs to serve. Mix the remaining chopped greens with the oyster liquor, then add the makrut lime juice and lemon zest.

4 Chop the oyster meat into large dice and add to the seaweed-citrus mixture. Drizzle in the oil and stir to gently emulsify. Season with sea salt flakes and freshly ground black pepper.

5 Spoon a tablespoonful of the oyster tartare into each of the oyster shells and decorate with the reserved sea greens and the sesame seeds. Serve immediately.

CHEF'S TIP
You'll find the specific marine plants and seaweed suggested here in organic or Asian grocery shops, or online.

INGREDIENTS
4 large oysters, ideally Portuguese • 200ml (7fl oz/⅓ pint) buttermilk • 40g (1½oz) samphire • 40g (1½oz) codium seaweed (or see recipe introduction) • 20g (¾oz) green laver (or see recipe introduction) • 80g (2¾oz) rock samphire (or see recipe introduction) • 2 tablespoons makrut lime juice • 1 tablespoon finely grated unwaxed lemon zest • 2 tablespoons olive oil • 1 tablespoon sesame seeds • Sea salt flakes • Freshly ground black pepper

OYSTERS

The story of Portuguese oysters could fill a whole book, starting with the 16th century and the Portuguese caravels to Japan, which brought Iberian oysters with them to the Far East on their hulls. These days, we are all aware of oyster population crises and epizootic diseases, but here we want to highlight the efforts being made to expand the healthy and sustainable cultivation of the native shellfish once again.

PRODUCTION

At present there are two main oyster production areas in Portugal:

- **In the centre:** the Tagus estuaries and, predominantly, in the Sado area in the Setúbal peninsula.
- **To the south:** in the Ria Formosa Natural Park.

THE PORTUGUESE OYSTER

The oysters of the country are of a robust, hardy species that grows fast... and it is a fine oyster! Deep-shelled and with the perfect balance between flesh and sea water, Portuguese oysters have a quite distinctive flavour.

OYSTERS OF THE CENTRAL REGION

André Magalhães told us about the extraordinary oysters farmed not far from Lisbon by Célia Rodrigues and her company, Neptun Pearl. The estuary waters there are a mixture of fresh and salt water and very rich in organic matter, which leads to the distinctively sweet taste of the oysters. Célia's goal is to revive the biological and cultural heritage of the region by reintroducing the production of native Portuguese oysters, farmed using sustainable, non-intensive methods. Célia also supplies chefs and restaurants across the country with seaweeds of all kinds: the simple, invigorating, iodine flavour of her sea vegetables enhances seafood beautifully.

MIGAS,
ALENTEJO STYLE

SERVES **4** • PREPARATION: **30 MINUTES** • COOKING: **40 MINUTES** • MARINATING: **1 HOUR**

EQUIPMENT: **FOOD PROCESSOR**

Migas means 'crumbs'. This famous dish from the Alentejo region has bread at the heart of the recipe, accompanied here by lean pork. It's a hearty, typically Portuguese family dish.

1   Cut the pork into 2cm (¾ in) cubes. Blend half the garlic, the red pepper, chilli or *piri-piri* powder, paprika and coarse salt in a food processor until it forms a paste. Tip into a large bowl. Add the pork, stir, add the white wine, mix again, cover and leave in the refrigerator for at least 1 hour.

2   Cut the stale bread into thin slices and set aside.

3   Fry the lardons in a large dry pan until crisp. Add the marinated pork and its marinade and cook over a low heat for 15 minutes, stirring occasionally. When the meat is cooked through (cut through a larger piece to check that no pink meat remains) and the sauce has reduced, turn off the heat and leave to rest in a warm place.

4   Brown the remaining garlic in a separate frying pan in a little olive oil. Add the thin slices of bread to the pan.

5   Add water to cover halfway, then set over a medium heat, all the time crushing the bread slices down with a wooden spoon. When the bread has been reduced to a fairly smooth paste, turn it over several times in the pan, allowing a crust to form on all sides.

6   Arrange these migas with the pork on a serving platter with the orange wedges and scatter with the coriander. Serve immediately.

INGREDIENTS

500g (1lb 2oz) lean pork (preferably pork shoulder) • 7 garlic cloves, crushed • ½ red pepper, chopped • 1 teaspoon chilli powder, or *piri-piri* powder • 2 tablespoons paprika • 3 tablespoons coarse sea salt • 100ml (3½fl oz) white wine • 400g (14oz) stale farmhouse bread • 100g (3½oz) bacon lardons • Olive oil • 1 orange, cut into wedges • a few sprigs of coriander, chopped

QUEIJADAS
WITH GINJA

MAKES **8** • PREPARATION: **30 MINUTES** • COOKING: **1 HOUR**

EQUIPMENT: **CUPCAKE TIN, OR SMALL INDIVIDUAL ROUND MOULDS**

Soft sheep's milk cheese, the tang of cherries and the charming sweet-sour Portuguese ginja *liqueur made from morello cherries (see page 177) make this recipe completely addictive.*

1   **Prepare the compote:** set aside some of the cherries for serving. In a saucepan, bring the *ginja* liqueur to the boil with the remaining morello cherries, the jam sugar and the cinnamon stick. Skim off any surface foam, then reduce the heat and simmer for 15 minutes.

2   Remove the cherries with a slotted spoon and set aside in a jar.

3   Leave the pan on the heat and reduce the juice. When the texture becomes syrupy, remove from the heat and leave to cool. Pour the juice over the cherries in the jar, seal and set in the refrigerator.

4   Preheat the oven to 200°C (400°F), Gas Mark 6.

5   **For the cakes:** in a glass bowl, use a large fork to mash up the soft cheese. Add the sugar, flour and yeast and mix with a spatula.

6   Add the melted butter, eggs and lemon zest and mix until smooth. Divide the mixture between 8 hollows in a cupcake tin, or small individual moulds, and bake for 30 minutes.

7   Leave to cool before turning out of the tin or moulds. Arrange on plates and spoon around the morello cherry compote. Decorate with the reserved cherries and serve.

INGREDIENTS
FOR THE CHERRY COMPOTE
500g (1lb 2oz) pitted morello cherries • 100ml (3½fl oz) *ginja* (see recipe introduction) • 100g (3½oz) jam sugar (with added pectin) • 1 cinnamon stick

FOR THE CAKES
500g (1lb 2oz) sheep's milk soft cheese • 200g (7oz) caster sugar • 2 tablespoons plain flour • ½ × 7g (¼oz) sachet of fast-action dried yeast • 75g (2¾oz) salted butter, melted and slightly cooled • 5 eggs • finely grated zest of 1 unwaxed lemon

TRAGEDY COCKTAIL

MAKES **1** • PREPARATION: **10 MINUTES**

This cocktail is a reference to the book The Tragedy of the Street of Flowers *by the writer Eça de Queirós, who was very famous in Portugal in the late 19th century. The story takes place in the Rua das Flores. The protagonist lives in the very same building as André's Taberna... So André serves this cocktail to his guests as a tribute to the character. The photo shows an original early edition of the book.*

1   Cut the orange and lemon slices and the ½ lime into 6 pieces each.

2   Place the citrus fruit, sugar and mint in a large glass and crush with a pestle.

3   Fill the glass with ice cubes (or crushed ice) and pour in the *genever*, wine and triple sec.

4   Top up the glass with sparkling water and stir with a cocktail spoon. Serve immediately with a straw.

INGREDIENTS
1 orange slice • 1 lemon slice • ½ lime • 5 tablespoons brown sugar • 5 mint leaves • 40ml (1 ⅓fl oz) *genever* • 40ml (1 ⅓fl oz) sweet Muscat wine • 40ml (1 ⅓fl oz) triple sec liqueur • Sparkling water

PAP' AÇORDA

MODERNIZING THE CLASSICS

Manuela Brandão's restaurant is a must-visit in Lisbon. Established in 1981, it was first set up in the heart of the Bairro Alto and is now located above the famous Mercado da Ribeira (see page 296), in the Cais do Sodré district. In this meticulously decorated setting, a perfectly trained team and a beautifully designed menu create a unique experience. The chef brings us here a colourful and lively selection of her recipes, inspiring and historic at once, a glimpse into the soul of this generous and caring chef.

Manuela was keen to share her two recipes for typical Portuguese bread, an essential part of the nation's table.

GARLIC BREAD ROLLS

MAKES **12** • PREPARATION: **10 MINUTES** • COOKING: **10 MINUTES**

EQUIPMENT: **STAND MIXER**

1 Preheat the oven to 200°C (400°F), Gas Mark 6. Place a tray of water on the bottom shelf of the oven (to create steam).

2 Place all the ingredients in the bowl of a stand mixer fitted with the dough hook. Knead for 6–7 minutes.

3 Divide the dough into 12 equal pieces. Shape each piece into a ball and then stretch on each side to form a small pointed baguette (see the photograph overleaf for guidance on shaping). Slash each rolls along its length.

4 Bake for 9–10 minutes.

5 When baked and golden, remove from the oven and leave to cool.

INGREDIENTS
300g (10½oz) strong white bread flour • 7g (¼oz) fine salt • 6g (¼oz) fresh yeast • 2 crushed garlic cloves • 18g (⅔oz) plain yogurt • 150ml (5fl oz/¼ pint) water

SEEDED BREAD

MAKES **1 LOAF (ABOUT 12 SLICES)** • PREPARATION: **20 MINUTES** •
COOKING: **40 MINUTES** • RISING: **2 HOURS**

EQUIPMENT: **STAND MIXER**

1   Place all the ingredients (except the seeds and salt) in the bowl
    of a mixer fitten with the dough hook and mix on a low speed for
    10 minutes. Then knead on a slightly higher speed for 5 minutes.

2   Add the seeds and salt and mix to a smooth dough.

3   Remove and leave to rise, covered, for 1 hour.

4   Knead the dough by hand briefly, then shape into a long baguette shape
    and leave to rise for a further 1 hour.

5   Preheat the oven to 200°C (400°F), Gas Mark 6. Slash the loaf along its
    length, then bake for 40 minutes.

6   When baked and golden, remove from the oven and leave to cool.

INGREDIENTS
600g (1lb 5oz) strong wholemeal flour • 300g (10½oz) rye flour • 330g (11½oz) polenta •
12g (⅖oz) fresh yeast • 90ml (6 tablespoons) water • 65g (2½oz) flax seeds •
65g (2½oz) sesame seeds • 25g (1oz) fine salt

OXTAIL BROTH
WITH PORT
FRENCH TOAST

SERVES **4 AS A STARTER** • PREPARATION: **2½ HOURS** • COOKING: **1 HOUR 5 MINUTES** • SALTING: **2 HOURS**

Manuela's version of açorda – that traditional stale bread and soup combo – is combined here with traditional Port wine. Whatever the season, and whatever your taste buds fancy, this recipe is comforting, drawing on the real fundamentals of Portuguese cuisine.

1   Place the oxtail on a bed of coarse salt in a tray and sprinkle the salt all over as well. Cover and set aside for 2 hours.

2   Wipe the oxtail clean of salt. Heat a little oil in a casserole dish, sear the oxtail on all sides, then add the onion, carrot, bay leaf and leek and cook, stirring, until the onion is translucent. Add water to just cover and simmer for 1 hour, covered, over a low heat.

3   Remove the oxtail, discard the fat and shred the meat from the bones using 2 forks.

4   Strain the broth, discarding the solids, then bring it to the boil in a saucepan. Add the vermicelli and cook for 4–5 minutes.

5   Add the shredded oxtail to the broth.

6   Dip the bread slices in a bowl with the milk and beaten egg. Heat a frying pan with a little olive oil, then add the bread slices. Once golden brown on both sides, drizzle with Port. Leave over a low heat for 2 minutes.

7   Place the French toast in warmed shallow bowls, ladle over the broth, the oxtail and the vermicelli, then top with a few mint leaves.

INGREDIENTS
150g (5½oz) oxtail • Coarse sea salt • Olive oil • 1 onion, chopped • 1 carrot, chopped • 1 bay leaf • ½ leek, chopped • 20g (¾oz) vermicelli • 4 slices of dry bread • 100ml (3½fl oz) milk • 1 egg, lightly beaten • ½ glass Port • A few mint leaves

BREAD

The history of Portuguese bread takes us back to the beginnings of maize cultivation in the country at the end of the 15th century. Maize was a main ingredient of the nation's bread (and these days we are all familiar with cornbread). However, Portuguese bread embraces a spectrum of flavours.

A LITTLE LANGUAGE LESSON

In Portugal, the word *broa* refers to bread made from maize or rye (mainly in the north). Whereas, in the south of Portugal, they use the word *pão*, derived from the Latin *panis*, which means 'bread' in general.

PORTUGUESE BREADS

- **Pão alentejano:** a large loaf with a compact crumb, generally used for *açordas* or *migas* (see pages 15, 119 and 139).
- **Pão de centeio:** dark-coloured bread made from rye flour, rich in fibre.
- **Pão de Mafra:** bread made from wheat and rye flour, the dough for this contains a lot of water, giving it a soft crumb and a firm crust. It is said to be a descendant of the ancient farmhouse breads traditionally baked around Lisbon.
- **Papo-seco or carcaça:** a bread roll made from wheat flour. All the different types of *bifana* sandwiches (see pages 35 and 167) are made with these rolls.
- **Broa de Avintes:** a real stand-out, traditional bread from the towns of Avintes and Vila Nova de Gaia, close to Porto. Brown, dense and slightly bittersweet, it is made with maize and rye flours. This is the bread André serves at his Taberna da Rua das Flores (see pages 97–123).

Of course, there are a myriad other types of bread, such as *bôla de carne* (filled with leftover meat and various types of sausage) or *pão com chouriço*.

AÇORDA ROYALE

SERVES **4** • PREPARATION: **30 MINUTES** • COOKING: **25 MINUTES**

Manuela Brandão's açorda royale is all about generosity and exceptional produce, as well as elegance. That's what characterizes the delicate version given here. She elevates a typical dish based on bread, stock, garlic and egg to new heights of refinement...

1   Soak the bread in a small bowl in the measured water until all the liquid has been absorbed.

2   Meanwhile, in a frying pan, fry the garlic in the oil until golden.

3   Heat the wet bread in a saucepan over a low heat and add a pinch of salt, most of the coriander (reserve a few sprigs) and the garlic. Mix to combine and cook over a low heat for 15 minutes, stirring constantly and adding more water if necessary: you are looking for a soup with a thick consistency.

4   Bring a large saucepan of water with the vinegar to the boil. Poach the eggs for 3 minutes (see page 15).

5   Place the bread and soup in a tureen with the poached eggs, prawns, lobster and reserved coriander.

6   Adjust the seasoning and serve.

CHEF'S TIP

Pão alentejano is a traditional bread made with natural yeast. It has a slightly acidic aftertaste, a compact crumb and a thick rustic crust. The special taste of this bread comes from its leavening and long fermentation time. It's an absolutely typical taste of Portugal and its traditions and can be found on every table, from north to south.

INGREDIENTS

400g (14oz) *alentejano* bread, or white farmhouse bread • 500ml (18fl oz) water • 6 garlic cloves, crushed • 50ml (2fl oz) olive oil • 100g (3½oz) bunch of coriander • 3 tablespoons white wine vinegar • 4 eggs • 12 cooked prawns, whole and shelled • 100g (3½oz) lobster meat • Salt and freshly ground black pepper

GREEN BEAN
TEMPURA

SERVES **4 AS A STARTER** • PREPARATION: **30 MINUTES** • COOKING: **20 MINUTES** •
CHILLING: **AT LEAST 1 HOUR**

Everyone knows tempura, which was exported by the Portuguese in the 16th century to Japan, and has now come back again. This simple, delicious recipe is perfect for serving with aperitifs, or as a starter with a few condiments.

1   Clean the green beans, remove the strings and cook in a saucepan of boiling salted water for 10 minutes. Strain over a bowl. Set aside the cooking water to chill in the refrigerator.

2   Pour the flour into a separate bowl and season with salt and white pepper, then add the egg, a good dash of olive oil and 200ml (7fl oz/⅓ pint) of the chilled cooking water. Mix to a smooth paste.

3   Heat a frying pan half-filled with vegetable oil, until a drop of the batter sizzles immediately when thrown in. Dip the green beans, one at a time, into the batter, allowing some of the batter to drip off, then drop into the oil in batches, so as not to overcrowd the pan, frying on all sides until golden brown.

4   Remove the beans from the oil with a slotted spoon and place on a plate lined with kitchen paper, to blot off excess oil, then serve immediately, sprinkled with sea salt flakes.

CHEF'S TIP
A good way of knowing when the batter is at the correct consistency is to test it by sticking in a clean finger. If it coats your finger, it's good!

INGREDIENTS
200g (7oz) green beans • 100g (3½oz) plain flour • 1 egg • Olive oil • Vegetable oil, to deep-fry • Salt and freshly ground white pepper • Sea salt flakes

JOHN DORY FILLETS
WITH ORANGE SAUCE

SERVES **4** • PREPARATION: **30 MINUTES** • COOKING: **15 MINUTES**

This recipe is a love story to Portugal. John Dory, a real hero of the nation's fisheries, is accompanied by the flagship citrus fruit of southern Europe: the orange. The result is strikingly fresh and delicious.

1   Season the John Dory fillets with salt, pepper and lemon juice. Zest the orange using a zester and juice it.

2   Put the flour on a plate and heat a frying pan with a drizzle of oil. Flour the fillets and gently fry them in the pan for 2 minutes on each side. Add the orange juice, zest and the crème fraîche. Bring to the boil for 5 minutes, then adjust the seasoning.

3   Place the fish fillets on a plate and drizzle the orange sauce over them.

4   Sprinkle with parsley leaves and serve with greens, plain boiled potatoes or rice.

INGREDIENTS
400g (14oz) John Dory fillets • Juice of 1 lemon • 1 organic orange • 10g (¼oz) plain flour • Olive oil • 100ml (3½fl oz) crème fraîche • A few parsley leaves • Salt and freshly ground black pepper

SALT COD SALAD
WITH ORANGE

SERVES **4 AS A STARTER** • PREPARATION: **30 MINUTES** • COOKING: **25 MINUTES** •
SOAKING: **24 HOURS**

A fresh and colourful starter, highlighting that quintessential Portuguese ingredient: salt cod. Quick and tangy, this is a recipe that's ideal for spring.

1 Desalinate the cod for 24 hours in a bowl of water placed in the bottom of the refrigerator, changing the water 2–3 times during the soaking. Drain off the soaking water.

2 Place the cod in a wide saucepan of fresh cold water. Heat until the water is simmering, then turn off the heat and leave the cod to poach in the residual heat for 20 minutes. Drain. Once cold, flake the cod, removing the skin and bones.

3 Place the flaked cod, orange segments, garlic and onion in a salad bowl.

4 Dress with the vinegar and olive oil, season with salt (if needed, as the cod will be salty) and scatter with parsley leaves. Serve immediately.

INGREDIENTS
400g (14oz) salt cod • 1 orange, segmented • 1 garlic clove, finely chopped • ¼ red onion, finely sliced • 1 tablespoon white wine vinegar • 3 tablespoons olive oil • A few parsley leaves • Salt

SALT COD

Salt cod – *bacalhau* – is undoubtedly Portugal's favourite ingredient. But it's so much more than that. These dried fillets tell the tale of an epic journey down through the ages, when seafarers battled the high seas, the cold and the challenges of international trade between the old and new worlds.

COD FISHING

Cod fisheries grew exponentially during the Age of Discovery. A map dating from 1524 shows that Portugal had already established trade routes to Newfoundland and Nova Scotia, where they were among the first Europeans to fish for cod. From the 15th to the 19th centuries, the number of cod fishermen on the Newfoundland route steadily rose, but these cold seas were eventually over-fished.

However, Portugal has always maintained the art of traditional fishing with lines in small boats. Nowadays - once again in the cold waters of northern Europe - cod is making a comeback. César De Sousa, chef of Pássarito in Paris (see pages 33 and 295) should know, and he told us he buys his best cod from Norway.

PREPARATION

To make *bacalhau*, cod is dried and salted so it can be preserved for a long time outside the refrigerator, if kept in a cool place and well wrapped in thick paper. If previously desalinated, it can also be frozen.

RECIPES

They say there are 365 ways of preparing *bacalhau*: one for each day of the year! Baked in the oven; cooked gratin-style with a bechamel sauce; sautéed with potatoes, onions and eggs... Desalinated salt cod can also be prepared as a simple steamed fish fillet. In Portugal, you'd be hard-pressed to find a restaurant that doesn't offer a *bacalhau* dish, or a family that hasn't eaten it in the last week.

BLACK PORK FILLET

WITH PAPRIKA, CORNBREAD PURÉE AND CHOURIÇO

SERVES **4** • PREPARATION: **30 MINUTES** • COOKING: **25 MINUTES** • MARINATING: **2 HOURS**

The most highly regarded Portuguese pork comes from the Iberian black pig, called porco preto, *which occupies pride of place in the country's meat cookery.*

1   Crumble the cornbread into a bowl, pour over the milk and leave to soak.

2   For the marinade, combine the white wine, paprika, bay leaf and garlic in a bowl and season with salt and pepper. Add the pork fillet. Mix well and leave to marinate, covered, for around 2 hours.

3   Heat the oil in a large frying pan, then add the pork fillet and marinade and cook slowly for 15 minutes. Adjust the seasoning if required.

4   Once soaked, mash the cornbread and milk in a bowl with a fork.

5   In a dry frying pan, fry the *chouriço* with the cornbread mixture until nicely browned.

6   Slice the pork fillet and arrange on a plate, then top with the *chouriço* and bread mixture. Serve with turnip greens or mashed potato and scatter with coriander leaves.

INGREDIENTS

150g (5½oz) cornbread • 100ml (3½fl oz) milk • 200ml (7fl oz/⅓ pint) white wine • 2 tablespoons paprika • 1 bay leaf • 2 garlic cloves, crushed • 400g (14oz) black pork fillet • 200ml (7fl oz/⅓ pint) olive oil • 200g (7oz) *chouriço*, finely chopped • Handful of coriander leaves • Salt and freshly ground black pepper

EGG AND VINEGAR
CUSTARD

SERVES **6** • PREPARATION: **30 MINUTES** • COOKING: **10 MINUTES**

EQUIPMENT: **PROBE THERMOMETER**

There have been whole books written about Portuguese desserts. Many are made using eggs, usually egg yolks. This contemporary twist on a traditional recipe combines the yolks with vinegar, adding a dash of acidity to balance the sweetness.

1 Bring the milk and fennel seeds to the boil in a large saucepan. Once it has boiled, strain the milk through a fine sieve into a clean saucepan and discard the fennel seeds. Add the vinegar and leave to stand away from the heat for around 10 minutes without stirring, until the milk coagulates.

2 Add the sugar to the milk, return to the heat and boil until it reaches 104°C (220°F) on a probe thermometer, 4–5 minutes.

3 In a bowl, whisk the egg yolks and whole egg with a little of the milk mixture to obtain a smooth blend. Pour back into the milk mixture in the pan.

4 Return the saucepan to a low heat, stirring constantly, until the mixture becomes thicker.

5 Leave to cool, then spoon into small serving glasses. Dust with cinnamon to serve.

INGREDIENTS

650ml (20fl oz) whole milk • 10g (¼oz) fennel seeds • 1 tablespoon white wine vinegar • 650g (1lb 7oz) caster sugar • 12 egg yolks • 1 whole egg • 1 teaspoon ground cinnamon

TANGY MANDARIN
CRÈME CARAMELS

SERVES **6** • PREPARATION: **15 MINUTES** • COOKING: **45 MINUTES**

EQUIPMENT: **6 INDIVIDUAL SAVARIN OR RUM BABA MOULDS**

Beautifully sunny yellow crowns!

1   Put 100g (3½oz) of the sugar in a light-coloured saucepan (so you can easily see the colour of the caramel). Place over a low heat and wait for the sugar to melt, then watch – swirling the pan now and then but not stirring – until it is golden brown. Pour this caramel into 6 individual savarin or rum baba moulds, swirling them to coat.

2   Preheat the oven to 200°C (400°F), Gas Mark 6. Whisk the whole eggs and yolks with the remaining sugar in a bowl. Add 140ml (4¾fl oz) of the mandarin juice, then strain through a sieve. Add the mandarin zest and pour the mixture into the moulds.

3   Put the moulds in a deep roasting tin and add hot water from the kettle to the tin to reach halfway up the sides of the moulds, being careful not to splash it into the caramels. Bake in the oven for 45 minutes until firm.

4   Cool, then upturn the moulds on to plates and serve, scattered with mandarin zest, if you like.

INGREDIENTS
240g (8½oz) caster sugar • 8 whole eggs • 2 egg yolks • Finely grated zest and juice of 2 organic mandarins, plus more zest (optional) to serve

NAVET SAUTÉES

BLOOD SAUSAGE

CRÈME BRULÉE

TOUCINHO DO CÉU

SERVES **6** • PREPARATION: **45 MINUTES** • COOKING: **45 MINUTES**

EQUIPMENT: **20CM (8IN) SPRINGFORM CAKE TIN** • **PROBE THERMOMETER**

Toucinho do céu *means 'bacon from heaven' and is a very old Portuguese recipe for a rich almond cake, here accompanied by pears poached in wine.*

1 For **the cake:** boil the measured water and sugar in a pan until it reaches 107°C/225°F on a probe thermometer. Stir in the squash jam. When it returns to the boil, add the almonds and cook, stirring, for 5 minutes.

2 Preheat the oven to 200°C (400°F), Gas Mark 6. Butter and flour a 20cm (8in) springform cake tin.

3 Whisk the egg yolks and whole egg in a bowl and season. Stir the eggs into the sugar and jam mixture to obtain a uniform consistency and cook until it comes away from the edges of the pan. Pour into the prepared tin and bake for 7–8 minutes, or until firm to the touch. Allow to cool, before removing from the tin.

4 **Prepare the pears in wine:** peel the pears. In a saucepan, mix all the ingredients except the pears. When it comes to the boil, add the pears and leave to simmer for 20–25 minutes. Leave to cool, then slice.

5 Serve the cake with the poached pears, drizzled with the red wine syrup.

CHEF'S TIP
You can find squash jam – doce de gila – in Portuguese grocery stores.

INGREDIENTS

FOR THE CAKE
500ml (18fl oz) water • 270g (9¾oz) caster sugar • 80g (2¾oz) squash jam (*doce de gila,* see chef's tip, above) • 110g (3¾oz) ground almonds • Butter, for the tin • Plain flour, for the tin • 9 egg yolks • 1 whole egg • Salt and freshly ground black pepper

FOR THE PEARS
3 William pears • 350ml (12fl oz) red wine • 50g (1¾oz) caster sugar • 2 cinnamon sticks • 2 cloves • 1 tablespoon cardamom pods • 1 tablespoon ground anise seeds

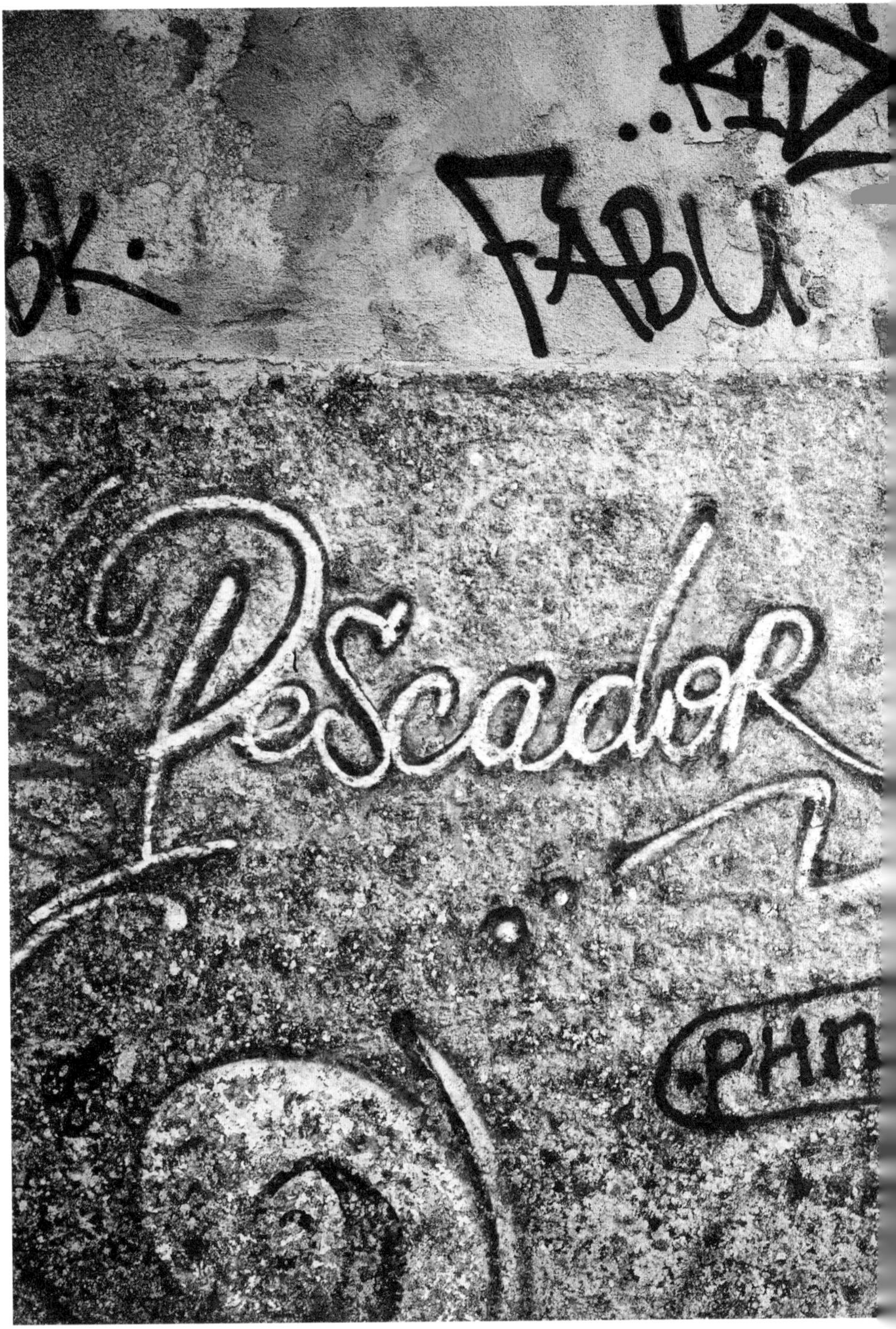
FABU
Pescador

CERVEJA MUSA

A CHEEKY NEW TWIST

The story of Musa microbrewery is much more than the tale of two friends getting together and deciding to make a Portuguese craft beer, though it's that as well. Bruno Carrilho and Nuno Dantas Melo brew their range of beers in Lisbon's Marvila district and now have four bars in the city. In their HQ (where you'd think you were in Brooklyn) they explained how they're all about the careful sourcing of ingredients from Portugal and elsewhere in Europe, expertly researched branding and skilfully honed flavours. And of course they were happy to concoct a few recipes for us to try, all containing beer, of course!

MUSA CHICKEN WINGS

SERVES **4** • PREPARATION: **10 MINUTES** • COOKING: **30 MINUTES** • MARINATING: **2 HOURS**

EQUIPMENT: **DEEP FRYER • PROBE THERMOMETER (BOTH OPTIONAL)**

A great dish that shouts of happy evenings out with friends. Bruno and Nuno rock this slow-cooked version with a 100 per cent IPA marinade. Fiery, revolutionary and fun!

1 **For the chicken:** trim the ends of the wings and discard, or use to make stock. Put them in a freezable container, pour over the IPA, cover and marinate for at least 2 hours in the freezer.

2 Pat the chicken wings dry with kitchen paper. Mix the cornflour, flour and garlic powder in a bowl, add the wings and mix to coat them in the flour.

3 Heat a deep fryer to 110°C/230°F, or heat the vegetable oil in a deep pan and check for the correct temperature with a probe thermometer. Working in batches so as not to overcrowd the pan, fry the chicken for 5 minutes to cook it through, then remove with a slotted spoon.

4 Now heat the oil to 180°C (350°F), or until a piece of the flour mixture, when thrown in, sizzles immediately. Fry for a further 10 minutes until the wings are golden brown. Remove from the oil with a slotted spoon, drain on kitchen paper and sprinkle with sesame seeds.

5 **To make the sauce:** mix everything together and serve with the wings.

INGREDIENTS

FOR THE CHICKEN
340g (12oz) chicken wings • 100ml (3½fl oz) Musa IPA beer • 35g (1¼oz) cornflour • 35g (1¼oz) strong white bread flour • Pinch of garlic powder • Vegetable oil, to deep-fry • Handful of sesame seeds

FOR THE SAUCE
1 teaspoon soy sauce • 1 garlic clove, finely chopped • 1 tablespoon sriracha • 1 tablespoon honey • Juice of 2 limes • 1 teaspoon peeled and grated root ginger • 1 teaspoon salt

SWORDFISH
BIFANAS

MAKES **4** • PREPARATION: **30 MINUTES** • COOKING: **15 MINUTES** • MARINATING: **2 HOURS**

A traditional recipe, remixed especially for us! A bifana is a typically Portuguese sandwich, made with white bread and thin slices of meat, marinated in garlic and bay leaves. Here, our duo from Musa have concocted a fresher version, using finely sliced marinated swordfish seasoned with coriander, with tangy escabeche vegetables on the side. The classic snack makes a delicious lunch to enjoy with a Mi Chela lager from the craft brewery.

INGREDIENTS
1 baguette, or 4 *carcaça* rolls

FOR THE SWORDFISH
150g (5½oz) swordfish fillets
50ml (2fl oz) Musa IPA beer
50ml (2fl oz) apple cider vinegar
Salt and freshly ground black pepper

FOR THE *SOFRITO*
½ red onion, finely chopped
1 garlic clove, finely chopped
4 teaspoons olive oil, plus more for the fish
1 bay leaf
1 mild red chilli, finely chopped

FOR THE *ESCABECHE* (MARINATED VEGETABLES)
4 tablespoons red wine vinegar
20g (¾oz) carrot, cut into matchsticks
20g (¾oz) yellow pepper, cut into matchsticks
20g (¾oz) red pepper, cut into matchsticks
4 tablespoons chilled IPA beer
A few coriander leaves, chopped (optional)

1 **Start with the fish:** cut the fillets into thin slices. Mix the beer and vinegar in a bowl, season well, add the fish and leave to marinate for 2 hours.

2 **Prepare the *sofrito*:** fry the onion and garlic in the oil with the bay leaf until the onion is soft and golden. Add the chilli and cook over a low heat for 5 more minutes, stirring.

3 **Make the *escabeche*:** add the vinegar to the *sofrito* and simmer gently.

4 Add the vegetables and simmer for 1 minute, then turn off the heat. Add the cold IPA, then transfer to a bowl, cover and chill the *escabeche* briefly (if you're short of time, pop it in the freezer for a few minutes while you finish the fish).

5 Heat a little oil for frying in a pan, add the swordfish slices and cook them for 1 minute on each side.

6 Cut the baguette (or rolls) in half lengthways and brush the *escabeche* pickling liquid on both halves. Add some of the vegetable matchsticks.

7 Arrange the swordfish on top and sprinkle over some chopped coriander, if you like. Cut the baguette, if using, into 4 pieces and serve with the rest of the *escabeche* on the side.

CHEF'S TIP
Carcaça is wheat flour bread and you must try it if you can find it in a Portuguese grocery store. It is the country's daily bread.

PICA-PAU
MUSHROOMS

MAKES **4 SHARING PORTIONS** • PREPARATION: **40 MINUTES** • COOKING: **40 MINUTES** •
INFUSING: **15 MINUTES** • STANDING: **2½ HOURS**

EQUIPMENT: **STAND MIXER • PROBE THERMOMETER**

Pica-pau – *which means skewered – is a sharing dish that is usually made with pork, but
Bruno and Nuno have used mushrooms here for a veggie twist. Enjoy with a Musa Twist and
Stout, or an IPA, or any beer you like!*

INGREDIENTS

FOR THE HIP-HOPPY BREAD ROLLS (MAKES 8)
15g (½oz) dried hops (pellets or cones)
300ml (10fl oz/½ pint) boiling water
400g (14oz) strong white bread flour
100g (3½oz) wholemeal flour
15g (½oz) salt
10g (¼oz) fast-action dried yeast
30g butter, melted

FOR THE PICA-PAU
4 teaspoons olive oil
1 bay leaf
200g (7oz) mushrooms, chopped into bite-sized pieces.
1 garlic clove, finely chopped
1 teaspoon Dijon mustard
150ml (5fl oz/¼ pint) Musa Twist and Stout, IPA or other
beer of choice
Juice of 1 lemon
Coriander leaves (optional)
Salt and freshly ground black pepper

1 **Make the rolls:** steep the hop pellets or cones in the measured boiling water for 15 minutes, then strain over a bowl and reserve the liquid.

2 Mix the 2 types of flour and the salt in the bowl of a stand mixer. Put the yeast in a bowl with 100ml (3½fl oz) of the hop infusion (at a temperature below 25°C/75°F when tested with a probe thermometer).

3 Add the yeast and the remaining hop infusion to the flour mixture and mix at low speed for 15 minutes. Add the melted butter, increase the speed to medium and mix for 5 minutes more. Cover and leave the dough to stand in a cool place for 30 minutes (it's fine to leave it in the mixer bowl).

4 Divide the dough into 8 × 100g (3½oz) balls, arrange them spaced well apart on a baking tray and leave to rise for 2 hours, until doubled in size.

5 Preheat the oven to as hot as it will go. Place the rolls in the oven and immediately reduce the temperature to 230°C (450°F), Gas Mark 8. Bake for 30 minutes.

6 **Now get on with the pica-pau:** heat the olive oil in a frying pan with the bay leaf. Add the mushrooms and garlic and cook until brown. Add the mustard and season with salt and pepper.

7 Add a dash of beer to the pan to deglaze it, scraping up the mustard and caramelized mushroom juices. Turn off the heat and stir in the remaining beer.

8 Transfer the mushrooms to a serving dish, drizzle the lemon juice over and scatter with coriander leaves, if you like.

WINES AND SPIRITS

Portugal has 190,000 hectares of vineyards and the country's wines are classified into four main categories: DOC, IPR, *vinhos regionais* and *vinhos de mesa*.

VINEYARDS AND APPELLATIONS

- **Vinho verde**, from the north of the country, is light, fresh and ideal with seafood and fish dishes.
- **Port**: the oldest PDO (Protected Designation of Origin) wine in the world, celebrated since 1756.
- The **Douro**: most wines here are made with red grape varieties, such as Tinta Roriz and Touriga Nacional. The Douro Valley is a UNESCO World Heritage site.
- **Dão**: a narrow valley where vines have been grown since the 12th century. The main grape is the renowned Touriga Nacional, which produces smooth, elegant wines.
- **Setúbal Peninsula**: this is where the best Muscat is produced.
- The **Bucelas** region, near Lisbon, is known as 'the Prince of Portuguese wine' and is famous for its dry white wines made from the Arinto grape. It was the only white wine in Portugal for many centuries.
- **The Alentejo region** produces some of Portugal's most powerful and finest wines. Castelo de Vide, Marvão, Portalegre, Crato and Alter do Chão are all wine-producing areas steeped in history, in the north of the Alentejo.

PORTUGUESE LIQUEURS

- *Medronho*: the small berries from the *Arbutus unedo* (strawberry tree) are fermented for at least a month, then distilled. After ageing in casks for around eight years, *medronho* – with an alcohol content of 40–50 per cent – is bottled.
- *Ginja* – also known as *ginjinha de Óbidos* – is a strong-tasting liqueur, flavoured with sweet-and-sour morello cherries. It dates back to the 17th century, when a monk spotted an opportunity to use the large quantities of fruit in this region, turning them into the well-known drink.

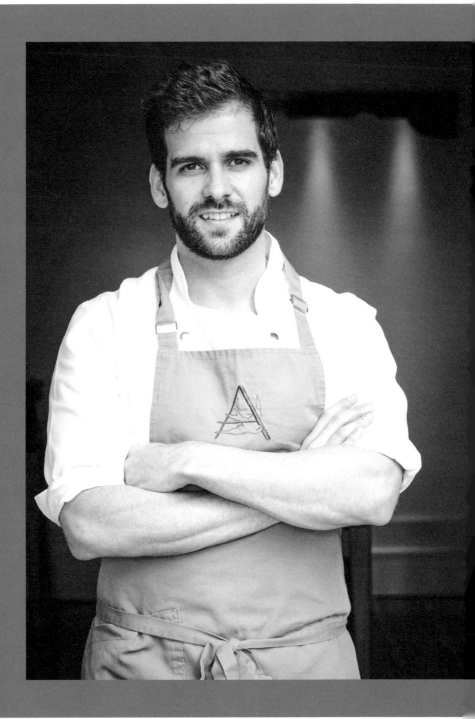

ALMEJA

CONTEMPORARY CUISINE

Porto, Portugal's second city, is brimming with talent and great places to eat, some modern, others more traditional. In Porto we met João Cura Mariano, chef at Almeja restaurant (see page 295). João belongs to the new generation of Portuguese chefs and has worked in many restaurants in the Iberian peninsula, notably Barcelona, the city globally famous for its experimental cuisine, before a desire to return to his roots drew him back to Portugal. A few months later, Almeja – literally 'longed for' – opened its doors. João's cooking feels like a distillation of childhood memories and walks by the sea and is inspired by the seasons, the producers he meets and the art of fermentation, in all its shapes and forms.

PORK TERRINE TOASTS

SERVES **6–8** • PREPARATION: **2 HOURS** • COOKING: **1 HOUR**

EQUIPMENT: **FOOD PROCESSOR** • **PROBE THERMOMETER**

For this recipe, I recommend buying a very good pig's head terrine.

INGREDIENTS
400g (14oz) pig's head terrine
(or brawn)

FOR THE AIOLI
1 garlic bulb
Pinch of saffron threads
1 tablespoon lemon juice
1 egg
Olive oil
Salt

FOR THE CARROT *ESCABECHE*
(OPTIONAL)
1 garlic clove, chopped
500g (1lb 2oz) onions, chopped
125g (4½oz) carrots, chopped
Olive oil
1 bay leaf
Sprig of thyme
Sprig of rosemary
200ml (700ml/⅓ pint) white
balsamic condiment

FOR THE GRANNY SMITH JELLY
100g (3½oz) freshly juiced Granny
Smith apple juice
100g (3½oz) caster sugar
100ml (3½fl oz) water
3g (scant ⅛oz) citric acid
2 teaspoons apple cider vinegar
4g (⅛oz) agar-agar

TO SERVE
250ml (9fl oz) balsamic vinegar
4 slices of bread
2 Granny Smith apples
Knob of butter
A few sprigs of herbs and/or
edible flowers

1 **Prepare the aioli:** preheat the oven to 200°C (400°F), Gas Mark 6. Wrap the whole garlic bulb in baking parchment, then in foil, and roast in the oven for 30–40 minutes. Squeeze the roasted garlic from the cloves into the bowl of a food processor and add the saffron, lemon juice, egg and a pinch of salt. Turn on the food processor to medium and gradually stream in olive oil until you have a mayonnaise. Transfer the aioli to a bowl and set aside.

2 **Prepare the carrot *escabeche* (if making):** cook the vegetables in a frying pan with the olive oil and the herbs until browned. Add the white balsamic and cook, stirring, until the vegetables are soft and tender. Set aside to cool.

3 **Prepare the Granny Smith jelly:** gently heat all the jelly ingredients until they reach 85°C (185°F) on a probe thermometer. Strain into a bowl and leave to cool. Once it becomes gelatinous, which it will when it is cold, blend it in the clean food processor, then set aside.

4 Reduce the balsamic vinegar by half in a saucepan over medium heat.

5 **To serve:** cut the pig's head terrine into 10 × 4cm (4 × ¼in) rectangles. Slice the bread into pieces the same size, then slice the apples into pieces the same width. Brown the bread in a frying pan with the knob of butter.

6 Assemble the toasts on each plate: a slice of browned bread, apple pieces and finally the pig's head terrine. Decorate with the *escabeche*, if using, the apple jelly and aioli and sprinkle with a few sprigs of herbs and/or edible flowers, adding a drizzle of the reduced balsamic vinegar to the plate to act as both decoration and condiment.

MONDEGO BLACK RICE

SERVES **4** • PREPARATION: **30 MINUTES** • COOKING: **1 HOUR**

EQUIPMENT: **FOOD PROCESSOR**

Similar to the Spanish recipe for arroz negro, *this dish is an ode both to Iberian cuisine and to the delicious rice grown in Portugal. The most common variety is the short-grain* Carolino.

INGREDIENTS

FOR THE RICE
1 tablespoon butter, plus 1 knob of butter
1 shallot, finely chopped
½ green pepper, finely chopped
½ red pepper, finely chopped
1 teaspoon *pimentón de la Vera* (sweet smoked paprika)
Juice of 2 tomatoes
300g (10½oz) *Carolino* rice, or risotto rice
1 glass of white wine
1 litre (1¾ pints) fish stock
80g (2¾oz) skinless white fish fillets, finely chopped
2 tablespoons squid ink
25g (1oz) samphire (marsh or rock), chopped
A few chives, chopped
Salt

FOR THE AIOLI
1 garlic bulb
Pinch of saffron threads
1 tablespoon lemon juice
1 egg
Olive oil
Salt

1 **Prepare the aioli:** preheat the oven to 200ºC (400ºF), Gas Mark 6. Wrap the whole garlic bulb in baking parchment, then in foil, and roast in the oven for 30–40 minutes. Squeeze the roasted garlic from the cloves into the bowl of a food processor and add the saffron, lemon juice, egg and a pinch of salt. Turn on the food processor to medium and gradually stream in olive oil until you have a mayonnaise. Transfer the aioli to a bowl and set aside.

2 **Now for the rice:** heat the tablespoon of butter in a frying pan and sauté the shallot without browning. Add the peppers and cook over a low heat for 5 minutes.

3 Add the *pimentón* and tomato juice. Leave the liquid to reduce a little, then add the rice. Simmer for 4–5 minutes.

4 Pour in the white wine and allow it to evaporate. Add the stock a ladle at a time, waiting between each addition until the liquid has been absorbed. When the rice is almost cooked (it starts to take on a creamy consistency), add the fish, squid ink and samphire. Add the knob of butter, season with salt and mix.

5 Serve like a risotto with a dollop of aioli on the side and sprinkled with chopped chives.

SQUID FIDEUÀ

SERVES **4** • PREPARATION: **1½ HOURS** • COOKING: **2–3 HOURS**

EQUIPMENT: **FOOD PROCESSOR**

Chef Mariano brought back the essence of this dish from his regular trips to Spain and added some Portuguese touches, in reference to his origins in Coimbra.

INGREDIENTS

FOR THE NOODLES
250g (9oz) vermicelli
400ml (14fl oz) fish stock

FOR THE *PICADA*
1 tablespoon olive oil
4 tablespoons crumbled stale bread
1 garlic clove, chopped
A few coriander spriglets

FOR THE *SOFRITO*
3 garlic bulbs
750g fresh squid, cleaned and sliced
1kg (2lb 4oz) onions, finely chopped
500g (1lb 2oz) tomatoes, skinned (see page 83)
and finely chopped
65g (2½oz) pepper paste (*massa pimentão*, or see
chef's tip, overleaf)
1 tablespoon caster sugar
50ml (2fl oz) olive oil
Salt

FOR THE AIOLI
1 whole garlic head
Pinch of saffron
1 tablespoon lemon juice
Olive oil
Salt

1 Preheat the oven to 200°C (400°F), Gas Mark 6.

2 Place the vermicelli in the oven on a baking tray lined with baking parchment and bake until golden brown. Keep the oven on.

3 **Prepare the *picada*:** heat the oil in a frying pan and brown the stale bread. Transfer to a bowl, cool, then mix with the remaining ingredients for the *picada* and set aside.

4 **Prepare the *sofrito*:** wrap 4 garlic bulbs (including the bulb for the aioli) separately in foil and bake for 30–40 minutes.

5 Heat a wide pan of water – only enough to just-cover the squid pieces – with a little salt. When the water starts to simmer, add the squid and cook without stirring until it boils, then add the onions and cook for 4 minutes. Add the tomatoes and cook over a low heat for 30 minutes, stirring occasionally and splashing in just a little more water if the pan seems too dry: it should be thick. This slow-cooking will produce very tender squid.

6 Squeeze the roasted flesh from 3 garlic bulbs and add to the pan, with the pepper paste and sugar. Cook, stirring, for 30 minutes.

7 **Prepare the aioli:** Squeeze the roasted garlic from the cloves into the bowl of a food processor and add the saffron, lemon juice, egg and a pinch of salt. Turn on the food processor to medium and gradually stream in olive oil until you have a mayonnaise. Transfer to a bowl and set aside.

8 Remove the squid from the sauce, pat dry, then fry in a frying pan with the olive oil until golden.

9 In each of 4 warmed ovenproof dishes, or 1 large serving platter or tray, if you prefer, spoon on the *sofrito* and *picada*, then add the browned vermicelli. Pour in the stock and bake for 3 minutes. Scatter over the squid and bake for 3 minutes more. Garnish with the aioli and coriander and serve.

CHEF'S TIP
You can buy massa pimentão *from Portuguese food shops, or just blend a jar of roasted peppers.*

KID GOAT,
CHERVIL ROOT PURÉE,
CARROT AND PARSNIP

SERVES **4** • PREPARATION: **1 HOUR** • COOKING: **12½ HOURS** • SALTING: **2 HOURS**

EQUIPMENT: **FOOD PROCESSOR**

Kid goat is a very common meat in northern Portugal, particularly in Porto. Here, João offers an elaborate recipe, for which the kid is first salted.

1 **Prepare the salting mixture:** mix the goat in a large non-reactive dish with the sugar, paprika and salt. Cover and marinate for 2 hours.

2 Remove the goat from the salt, wiping it away, then place in an ovenproof dish with the olive oil and pepper. Bake in the oven for 12 hours at 75°C (165°F), Gas Mark ¼. Finish cooking at 220°C (425°F), Gas Mark 7 for a final 10 minutes.

3 **For the vegetables:** fry the parsnip ribbons in a pan with a drizzle of sunflower oil to make crisps.

4 **Make the purée:** Place the chervil roots and 100g (3½oz) butter in a frying pan and leave them to slowly caramelize fort 20 minutes, stirring regularly. Once cooked, add the cream, blend to a purée and season to taste.

5 In a separate frying pan, cook the baby carrots in the 20g (¾oz) butter with the thyme, lemon juice and a pinch of salt until tender. Serve the meat and its juices with the vegetables and purée.

INGREDIENTS

FOR THE KID GOAT AND SALTING MIXTURE
800g (1lb 12oz) goat leg, or kid goat leg, on the bone • 500g (1lb 2oz) caster sugar • 250g (9oz) paprika • 1kg (2lb 4oz) coarse sea salt • 1 tablespoon olive oil • 1 tablespoon freshly ground black pepper

FOR THE VEGETABLES
1 parsnip, cut into ribbons with a vegetable peeler • sunflower oil • 8 baby carrots, ideally heritage varieties • 20g (¾oz) butter • Sprig of thyme • Juice of 1 lemon

FOR THE CHERVIL ROOT PURÉE
1kg (2lb 4oz) chervil roots, peeled and chopped • 100g (3½oz) butter • 100g (3½oz) single cream • Salt

DECONSTRUCTED BANOFFEE

SERVES **4** • PREPARATION: **20 MINUTES** • COOKING: **35 MINUTES**

EQUIPMENT: **20CM (8IN) SQUARE CAKE TIN** • **PROBE THERMOMETER** • **PIPING BAG** •
FOOD PROCESSOR • **SILICONE BAKING MAT**

A labour of love, so save it for a special dinner for friends, but so much fun! This takes a well-known flavour combination to astonishing new heights. It's worth taking time to make the plates look beautiful, for maximum impact.

INGREDIENTS
4 scoops of white chocolate ice cream

FOR THE BANANA BREAD
50g (1¾oz) butter, melted, plus more for the tin
150g (5½oz) ground almonds
600g (1lb 5oz) ripe bananas, mashed
5 eggs, separated
200g (7oz) caster sugar

FOR THE BANANA PURÉE
75g (2¾oz) caster sugar
100g (3½oz) ripe bananas, sliced
50ml (2fl oz) double cream

FOR THE BANANA TUILE
130g (4½oz) banana purée (simply whizz ripe bananas
in a food processor)
350ml (12fl oz) water
15g (½oz) plain flour

FOR THE BUTTERSCOTCH SAUCE
375g (13oz) demerara sugar
500ml (18fl oz) double cream
60g (2¼oz) smooth peanut butter
2 tablespoons whisky
2 teaspoons salt
500ml (18fl oz) crème fraîche

1   Preheat oven to 190°C (375°F), Gas Mark 5. Butter a 20cm (8in) square cake tin and line it with baking parchment.

2   **Bake the banana bread:** in a mixing bowl, combine the ground almonds with the mashed banana and melted butter. Fold the egg yolks and sugar into the mixture. In a separate bowl, whisk the egg whites until stiff, then gently fold it into the batter. Pour the batter into the prepared tin and bake for 25 minutes, or until firm to the touch. When completely cool, cut into cubes.

3   **Prepare the banana purée:** place the sugar and 1 tablespoon of water in a saucepan over a medium heat. Stir until a golden caramel forms and thickens (about 5 minutes), then immediately add the sliced bananas and then the cream. Stir to combine, then blend with a stick blender until smooth. Set aside in a piping bag.

4   **Make the banana tuile:** mix the banana purée with the measured water and flour, then spread the mixture out on a silicone mat. When the cake is baked, reduce the oven temperature to 170°C (340°F), Gas Mark 3½ and bake the tuile for 15 minutes.

5   **Prepare the butterscotch sauce:** bring all the ingredients except the crème fraîche to the boil in a saucepan until the mixture reaches 109°C/228°F on a temperature probe. Add the crème fraîche and mix. Strain the mixture through a sieve into a bowl and leave to cool.

6   Place a quenelle of ice cream on each plate with cubes of banana bread and swirls of banana purée. Top with butterscotch sauce and place a shard of the banana *tuile* on top.

OLIVE OIL

Olive oil is an indispensible ingredient in Portuguese cuisine and is produced in six PDO (Protected Designation of Origin) regions of the country:

- **Trás-os-Montes**: north-east of the Porto region in the north of the country
- **Beira Interior**: in the central-eastern part of Portugal
- **Ribatejo**: following the course of the River Tagus, approaching Lisbon
- **Alentejo Interior**: to the south of Lisbon, the region with Portugal's largest olive oil production, where traditional farming methods are used
- **Norte Alentejano**: in the north of the Alentejo region
- **Moura**: in the south-east of the Alentejo region

OLIVE VARIETIES

- **Cobrançosa**: from the north and centre of Portugal. Oils extracted from these olives are complex and intense, characterized by grassy and apple notes, combining sweetness with a slight sensation of bitterness, even spiciness.
- **Cordovil**: mainly grown in the Alentejo region, this variety of olives produces oils with leaf, grass and green tomato notes. It is slightly bitter and spicy, and has a lingering fruitiness.
- **Galega**: the most abundant olive variety in Portugal and accounting for 80 per cent of production. The oils are sweet and dense, with apple notes.
- **Verdeal**: from the Alentejo and Trás-os-Montes regions, with very marked and persistent notes. The oils are green, with a slight bitterness.
- **Carrasquenha, also called Carrasca or Redonda:** grown in the Alentejo region, these are dual purpose oils, suitable both for cooking and for finishing dishes.
- **Maçanilha Algarvia**: grown in the Algarve region, this oil is appreciated for its very sweet and rounded aromas.

DID YOU KNOW...?

A century ago, debts in Portugal were paid in olive trees!

The best light olive oil in the world is produced in Ferreira in the Alentejo region: it won the Mario Solinas Prize, a coveted international industry award, in 2018.

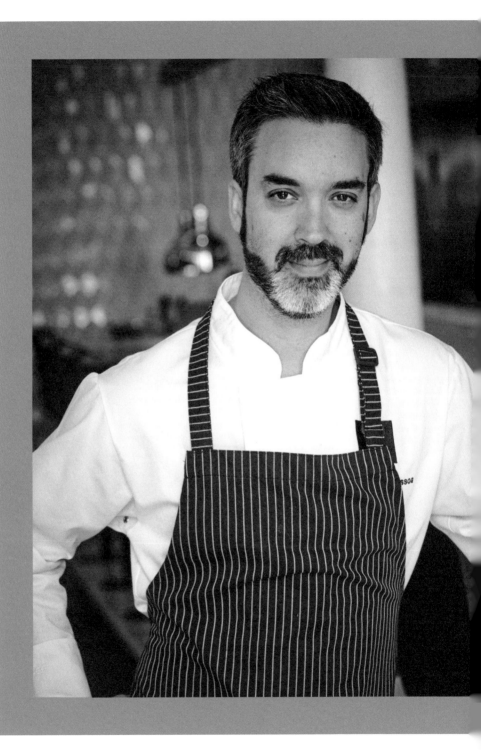

TABISCO

MODERN PETISCOS

Tapisco. The name conjures up images of Portuguese *petiscos*, the country's answer to tapas. This restaurant in Lisbon (see page 295) features the Portuguese sharing classics in a simple, fun and relaxed informal atmosphere. The food reflects a blend of cultures, influenced by the chef's career in the USA, London and Sydney, but underscored by his Portuguese origins. The chef, Henrique Sa Pessoa, is generous, welcoming and friendly and shares with us here four top recipes from his *Tapisco* menu.

TARTARE-STYLE
SALT COD

SERVES **4** • PREPARATION: **30 MINUTES** • COOKING: **1½ HOURS** • SOAKING: **24 HOURS**

EQUIPMENT: **RING MOULD OR PASTRY CUTTER**

A mild, smooth, melt-in-the-mouth dish, this is well-balanced comfort food, presented in the style of a traditional beef tartare, but showcasing Portugal's beloved salt cod. The egg confit and black olive make wonderful finishing touches. We love it and think you will, too.

INGREDIENTS

FOR THE TARTARE
400g (14oz) salt cod fillets
300g (10½oz) potatoes, cut into matchsticks
1 onion, finely chopped
1 garlic clove, finely chopped
1 bay leaf
4 tablespoons olive oil
3 eggs
2 tablespoons finely chopped parsley leaves
2 tablespoons finely chopped pitted black olives
Salt and freshly ground black pepper

FOR THE EGG YOLK CONFIT
4 egg yolks
100ml (3½fl oz) olive oil

1 **Start the tartare:** Desalinate the cod for 24 hours in a bowl of water placed in the bottom of the refrigerator, changing the water 2–3 times during the soaking. Drain off the soaking water.

2 Place the cod in a wide pan of cold water. Heat until simmering, then turn off the heat and leave the cod to poach in the residual heat for 20 minutes. Drain. Once cold, flake the cod, removing the skin and bones. Set aside.

3 Bring a saucepan of water to the boil and add the potato matchsticks. Cook for 12–15 minutes, then drain.

4 **To make the egg yolk confit:** place the yolks in an ovenproof dish and cover with the olive oil. Place them in an oven preheated to 70°C (160°F), Gas Mark ¼ and cook for 1 hour, carefully turning the yolks over halfway through. Set aside.

5 In a frying pan, sweat the onion, garlic and bay leaf in the olive oil over a low heat for 10–12 minutes. Add the flaked cod and cook for 1–2 minutes over a low heat. Remove from the heat and add half the cooked matchstick potatoes, season with salt and pepper and mix well.

6 Break the 3 whole eggs into the mixture and continue to cook over a low heat for 2–3 minutes. Add the remaining potatoes and mix again. The texture should be creamy, with slightly crispy potatoes.

7 Using a ring mould or pastry cutter, arrange the cod and potato mixture on plates, add the chopped parsley and top with the confit egg yolks and black olives.

OCTOPUS SALAD
WITH PEPPERS AND PAPRIKA

SERVES **4** • PREPARATION: **45 MINUTES** • COOKING: **40 MINUTES**

A staple of Portuguese cuisine: octopus. This version is a fantastic combo of peppers and potatoes and works well either as a starter for six to eight or as a hearty main course. With just the right amount of paprika and onion to liven it up, it's a real treat.

1 Place the octopus in a cast-iron pan with just enough water to cover, bring to the boil and cook over a medium heat for 15 minutes. Drain, then cut into bite-sized sections.

2 In a bowl, mix the garlic, onion and peppers with the coriander, olive oil and vinegar. Season with salt and pepper.

3 Bring a saucepan of water to the boil. Cook the potatoes until tender (20–25 minutes, depending on their size). Once they are cooked, drain, allow to cool, then peel and cut into cubes.

4 In a separate bowl, mix the pieces of octopus, tomato and potato cubes. Mix with the pepper, garlic and onion mixture.

5 Arrange the octopus on plates with the smoked paprika. Decorate with micro herbs, if you like, then serve.

INGREDIENTS
400g (14oz) octopus tentacles • 1 garlic clove, finely chopped • ½ red onion, finely chopped • ½ red pepper, finely chopped • ½ green pepper, finely chopped • 2 tablespoons chopped coriander • 6 tablespoons olive oil • 2½ tablespoons red wine vinegar • 200g (7oz) potatoes, scrubbed but unpeeled • 1 tomato, skinned (see page 83) and finely chopped • 1 teaspoon smoked paprika • A few micro herbs (optional) • Salt and freshly ground black pepper

OCTOPUS

The octopus appears EVERYWHERE in Portugal: on tiles, in murals and, of course, on plates. It's mostly caught in the region between Lisbon and the Algarve and there are countless ways to prepare it. In summer, people love *salada de polvo*.

A DISH OF CHOICE

Octopus is eaten throughout Portugal; in the past, it was dried to preserve it. These days, it is sold fresh and, more often than not, frozen, which also tenderizes the flesh. In coastal regions, it's not unusual still to see octopus drying outside fishermen's houses. It is delicious, as long as you know how to cook it. And they certainly do in Portugal.

CHEF'S TIPS

There are a few basic rules to follow when cooking octopus:

• Preferably buy fresh.

• Don't add salt until the octopus is fully cooked.

• The larger the octopus, the tougher its flesh: go for small octopus if you can.

• There are several ways to cook it: in a pressure cooker, a steamer, in stock, seared on a *plancha* or in a frying pan.

• If you choose to cook octopus in stock, prick the flesh all over.

OCTOPUS CARPACCIO

This is an original way to enjoy octopus: take a plastic bottle and remove the neck with a serrated knife so you are left with the main part. Put a cooked octopus inside the bottle and press it down to compress. Leave it for at least one night in the freezer, then cut away the bottle with scissors. You will have an octopus cylinder. Cut it into very thin slices and serve fanned out on plates as a carpaccio, with a light dressing of oil and white wine vinegar.

PEAS, EGGS
AND CHOURIÇO

SERVES **4 AS A STARTER** • PREPARATION: **20 MINUTES** • COOKING: **65 MINUTES**

EQUIPMENT: **PROBE THERMOMETER**

The Portuguese version of baked eggs. The freshness of the peas works well with the strong flavour of the chouriço and the warm tomato stock. A very simple recipe and an easy starter.

1 Cook the eggs in a saucepan of boiling water at 64°C/147°F for 45 minutes (the temperature needs to be exact for the cooking to be correct; you are essentially cooking them sous-vide without a machine). Lift out of the pan and set aside, keeping the pan over the heat.

2 In a frying pan, sauté the onion and garlic with the olive oil for 4–5 minutes. Add the *chouriço* and brown for a further minute.

3 Add the white wine and allow it to evaporate. Add the tomato purée, bay leaf and stock and bring to the boil.

4 Once simmering, add the peas, tomato and coriander. Season with salt and pepper and cook for 10 minutes over a low heat.

5 Carefully peel the eggs and reheat them by plunging them into the hot water they were cooked in.

6 Serve in 4 small individual dishes. Top each with an egg and sprinkle with micro herbs, if you like.

INGREDIENTS
4 eggs • ½ onion, finely chopped • 1 garlic clove, finely chopped • 4 tablespoons olive oil • 150g (5½oz) *chouriço*, sliced • 2 tablespoons white wine • 1 tablespoon tomato purée • 1 bay leaf • 200ml (7fl oz/⅓ pint) vegetable stock • 500g (1lb 2oz) peas • 1 tomato, chopped • 2 tablespoons finely chopped coriander • A few micro herbs (optional) • Salt and freshly ground black pepper

CHOCOLATE MOUSSE
WITH OLIVE OIL

SERVES **4–6** • PREPARATION: **20 MINUTES** • COOKING: **7 MINUTES** •
STANDING: **2 HOURS**

EQUIPMENT: **FOOD PROCESSOR**

We couldn't possibly end a good bistro menu in Portugal without a chocolate mousse: César (at Pássarito, see page 33) told us so. So I'd like to share this recipe, seasoned with local liquid gold for pure pleasure.

1   Melt the chocolate in a heatproof bowl set over a pan of shallow simmering water, being careful the bowl does not touch the water.

2   Mix the egg yolks and sugar in a food processor until the mixture turns pale, then gradually add the olive oil while blending, as you would for a mayonnaise.

3   In a clean bowl, whisk the egg whites until stiff.

4   Add the melted chocolate to the egg yolk mixture, then gradually fold in the whisked egg whites, trying to keep in all the air.

5   Divide the mixture between 4–6 glasses and leave to set in the refrigerator for at least 2 hours.

6   Before serving, finish with a little olive oil caviar, or just a drizzle of olive oil, and a large pinch of sea salt flakes.

INGREDIENTS
140g (5oz) 70 per cent cocoa solids chocolate, broken into pieces • 4 egg yolks • 80g (2¾oz) caster sugar • 4 tablespoons olive oil, plus more (optional) to serve • 5 egg whites • Olive oil pearls or caviar (optional) • large pinch of sea salt flakes

PRADO

THE CUTTING EDGE

This is contemporary Portuguese cuisine. António Galapito worked
for many years with the best-known Portuguese chef abroad – Nuno
Mendes in London – before deciding to return to Lisbon. In winter 2017,
he opened Prado restaurant, shortly followed by a delicatessen of the
same name just down the street (see page 295). It is modern cuisine
that reflects his travels, technically accomplished and bold.
The room is charming and so is the chef, who shares here his
resolutely modern dishes.

MACKEREL
IN VINAIGRETTE WITH PARSLEY AND SEA LETTUCE

SERVES **4** • PREPARATION: **1 HOUR** • COOKING: **25 MINUTES** • SALTING: **20 MINUTES**

EQUIPMENT: **HOT SMOKER • 2 TABLESPOONS BEECH WOOD CHIPS • BLENDER**

Mackerel version 2.0. António's dish is a state-of-the-art recipe: mackerel freshly smoked over beech wood, with a very green-flavoured vinaigrette of parsley and sea lettuce. It's surprising, it's full of flavour and it rocks.

1 Put the mackerel fillets in a non-reactive container, sprinkle over the coarse salt, set aside for 20 minutes, then rinse in cold water.

2 Place the sea lettuce, the 2 types of vinegar and the olive oil in a blender. Blend until very smooth.

3 Cook the parsley in a pan of boiling salted water for 3 minutes, then drain, transfer to a bowl of iced water and leave to cool. Set aside.

4 Drain the parsley once more and pat dry with kitchen paper, then blend until smooth, adding the garlic or grapeseed oil. Strain through a sieve.

5 For hot smoking, put 2 tablespoons of beech wood chips in the bottom of a hot smoker and place the fillets on the grill. Hot-smoke the fillets at about 40°C/104°F for 20 minutes, according to the manufacturer's instructions, then leave to cool.

6 Season the mackerel with the sea lettuce vinaigrette and serve the parsley emulsion on the side, with a few salad leaves.

CHEF'S TIP
If you don't have a smoker, ask your fishmonger or grocer for smoked mackerel fillets.

INGREDIENTS
2 good-sized mackerel, filleted • 2 tablespoons coarse sea salt • 50g (1¾oz) sea lettuce • 1 teaspoon apple cider vinegar • 1 teaspoon white wine vinegar • 4 tablespoons olive oil • 300g (10½oz) flat-leaf parsley • 2 teaspoons garlic oil, or grapeseed oil • Salad leaves • Salt

MUSSELS,
CHARD AND HERBS

SERVES **4** • PREPARATION: **30 MINUTES** • COOKING: **20 MINUTES**

EQUIPMENT: **STICK BLENDER**

Celebrate the sea with this simple, tasty shellfish dish. The slightly bitter notes of the chard bring balance to a very contemporary recipe.

1   Heat the olive oil in a large lidded pan, add the garlic cut-sides down and fry until the oil is redolent of garlic, but don't let it burn or it will be bitter. Discard any mussels that are open, then add the rest to the garlic oil and cover the pan. Cook for 10 minutes until the mussels open (discard any that remain closed). Strain, reserving the mussel juice and discarding the garlic. Remove the mussels from their shells and set aside.

2   Using a stick blender, emulsify the garlicky mussel juices with 150g (5½oz) of the butter.

3   In a frying pan, brown the bread in the remaining 20g (¾oz) butter over a low heat until crunchy outside but soft inside.

4   In a saucepan, bring the mussel emulsion to the boil, add the chard and cook for 30 seconds. Remove and set aside.

5   Reheat the mussels in the same sauce over a low heat for 5 minutes.

6   On each plate, arrange the pieces of fried bread, mussels, mussel sauce, chard and a few coriander leaves and serve.

INGREDIENTS
2 tablespoons olive oil • 1 garlic bulb, halved horizontally • 1kg (2lb 4oz) mussels, cleaned •
170g (6oz) butter • 200g (7oz) crustless farmhouse loaf, coarsely chopped •
200g (7oz) chard leaves • A few coriander leaves

MINHOTA BEEF TARTARE,
SHIITAKE AND BARBECUED CABBAGE

SERVES **4** • PREPARATION: **30 MINUTES** • COOKING: **10 MINUTES** • SMOKING: **2 HOURS**

EQUIPMENT: **COLD SMOKER** • **BARBECUE**

This is an astonishing recipe. Matured, smoked beef from Portugal's renowned Minhota cattle meets powerful barbecued cabbage and smooth shiitake mushrooms. Your guests won't believe you actually made this. But you did!

1   Cold-smoke the beef for around 2 hours, according to the manufacturer's instructions, then finely chop it.

2   Blanch the shiitake mushrooms for around 1 minute in a saucepan of boiling water. Remove them from the water with a slotted spoon, then pat dry with kitchen paper and slice them.

3   Blanch the cabbage leaves in the same water for 30 seconds. Leave to cool, then remove the central tough ribs from each leaf.

4   Mix the beef, sliced mushrooms, three-quarters of the beef fat and the egg yolks in a bowl, then add a pinch of salt and the chilli oil.

5   Brush the cabbage leaves with the remaining beef fat, then grill them on a barbecue until crunchy.

6   Place the beef tartare inside the cabbage leaves to serve.

INGREDIENTS
250g (9oz) very good-quality beef fillet, aged for at least 30 days • 50g (1¾oz) shiitake mushrooms •100g (3½oz) green cabbage leaves • 25g (1oz) beef fat • 3 egg yolks • 4 tablespoons chilli oil • Salt

SWEETBREADS,
SHELLFISH SAUCE AND WATERCRESS

SERVES **4** • PREPARATION: **1 HOUR** • COOKING: **1 HOUR** • BRINING: **2 HOURS** •
STANDING: **10 MINUTES**

EQUIPMENT: **PROBE THERMOMETER • BARBECUE**

António's version of surf and turf, featuring a sauce of prawns with tangy whisky notes against the bitterness of watercress. Ask your fishmonger to get you prawn heads and shells.

1   In a saucepan, bring the beef stock to the boil. Plunge the sweetbreads in and blanch for around 20 seconds, then transfer to a bowl of iced water and leave to cool. Clean the sweetbreads by peeling away the membrane.

2   Make a brine by mixing the salt and measured water in a non-reactive bowl. Add the sweetbreads, cover and leave for 2 hours. Drain the sweetbreads, pat dry with kitchen paper and set aside.

3   In a frying pan, cook the prawn heads and shells in a drizzle of olive oil for 15 minutes over a low heat, then add the whisky and flambé with a long-handled match, or by tipping the pan towards the flame. Once the whisky has evaporated, add water to cover and simmer for a further 25 minutes over a low heat.

4   Add the butter, mix, then pour the sauce through a sieve into a clean saucepan. Set aside and keep warm.

5   On the barbecue, grill the sweetbreads gently and slowly, turning them every minute to cook evenly on both sides until they reach 66°C (150°F) in the centre. Once grilled, leave to stand for around 10 minutes.

6   Arrange the sweetbreads on warmed plates and add the prawn sauce and a few watercress leaves to serve.

INGREDIENTS
200ml (7fl oz/⅓ pint) beef stock • 500g (1lb 2oz) sweetbreads • 50g (1¾oz) salt •
1 litre (1¾ pints) water • 500g (1lb 2oz) of prawn heads and shells • olive oil •
100ml (3½fl oz) whisky • 30g (1oz) butter, cut into pieces • 100g (3½oz) watercress

STRAWBERRIES,
SEA LETTUCE GRANITA AND BLACK PEPPER MERINGUE

SERVES **4** • PREPARATION: **20 MINUTES** • COOKING: **1 HOUR 10 MINUTES** •
FREEZING: **2 HOURS**

EQUIPMENT: **FOOD PROCESSOR • SILICONE BAKING MAT**

Contemporary cuisine enters the dessert realm. Here, strawberries encounter the bitterness of sea lettuce, a type of sea vegetable. The almost disconcertingly fresh granita cuts through the sweet strawberries and the rich glossy sauce. Throw in some crunchiness from meringue for good measure and you have a very successful dish.

INGREDIENTS
About 20 whole strawberries

FOR THE SEA LETTUCE GRANITA
200ml (7fl oz/⅓ pint) water
10g (¼oz) dried sea lettuce
30g (1oz) caster sugar

FOR THE STRAWBERRY SAUCE
250g (9oz) strawberries, hulled and cut into small pieces
10g (¼oz) caster sugar

FOR THE MERINGUE
6 egg whites
360g (12¼oz) icing sugar
Pinch of freshly ground black pepper

1   **Prepare the granita:** heat the measured water. Put the sea lettuce in a heatproof bowl, pour the water over it and leave to rehydrate for 5 minutes. Strain the liquid through a sieve into a bowl, add the sugar and mix until thoroughly combined. Pour into a large rimmed baking tray and place in the freezer for 2 hours.

2   **Prepare the strawberry sauce:** put the strawberry pieces and the sugar in a food processor and blend thoroughly. Set aside.

3   Preheat the oven to 150°C (300°F), Gas Mark 2.

4   **Prepare the meringue:** whisk the egg whites for 2 minutes at high speed until stiff. When they form peaks, add the icing sugar and pepper. Whisk again for 30 seconds.

5   Spread the meringue on a silicone baking mat laid in a baking tray, bake for 30 minutes, then reduce the oven temperature to 90°C (225°F), Gas Mark ¼ and cook for a further 40 minutes.

6   Remove the granita from the freezer. Scrape it over 4 bowls with a fork, then add the strawberry sauce. Cut the whole strawberries into quarters just before serving and add to the bowls with the crumbled meringue.

PORK FAT AND GARLIC
EMULSION

SERVES **4** • PREPARATION: **15 MINUTES** • COOKING: **1½ HOURS** • STANDING: **2½ HOURS**

In northern Europe, they happily spread butter on bread at the start of a meal. In Italy, they dip focaccia into olive oil. In Portugal, António introduced us to this lard (yes, you read that right) mixture flavoured with herbs. Delicious and unusual, I highly suggest you give it a try.

1   Preheat the oven to 140°C (275°F), Gas Mark 1.

2   Put all the ingredients except the salt and matcha powder in an ovenproof dish. Bake for 1 hour, then increase the oven temperature to 160°C (325°F), Gas Mark 3 for 30 minutes.

3   Strain the mixture through a sieve into a bowl and chill in the refrigerator for 2 hours. If you want to serve it with garlic, fry it in a little of the lard until golden.

4   Once the mixture has cooled, whisk until smooth, then add the sea salt flakes and mix them through.

5   Place the mixture in small individual ramekins, sprinkle over the matcha powder and chill for a further 30 minutes.

6   Serve sprinkled with the golden garlic, if you like, with sourdough bread.

| CHEF'S TIP
For this recipe, you really need to get hold of very good-quality lard, ideally the Alentejo type, or from Spanish jamón, available online.

INGREDIENTS
1kg (2lb 4oz) very good-quality lard (see chef's tip, above) • 1 tablespoon white peppercorns • 4 bay leaves • 1 garlic bulb, halved horizontally, plus 1 garlic clove (optional), finely chopped, to serve • 240ml (8fl oz) water • Pinch of sea salt flakes • 1 tablespoon matcha powder

CHEESE

High-quality Portuguese cheeses are generally made from sheep's and goat's milk. The main farming areas are around the Mondego River in the north, the Sado River in the south and the Guadiana River in the east. Portuguese cheese-making is still very much a cottage industry: many of the cheeses are produced by farmers and shepherds for their own consumption and relatively few are widely sold.

THE PDOS

Portugal has 15 PDO (Protected Designation of Origin) cheeses, including:

- *Queijo de Azeitão*
- *Queijo Rabaçal*
- *Queijo Serra da Estrela*
- *Queijo de Cabra Transmontano*

Other notable cheeses include *Alcobaça Leiria*, *Brandas de Cachena* and *Castelo de Vide*.

OUR THREE FAVOURITES

- *Queijo de Cabra Transmontano* comes from Bragança and Vila Real and is a hard cheese, made with goat's milk from mountainous regions. It is white and creamy, with a mild, sometimes slightly spicy flavour. It can be eaten grated or simply sliced.
- *Terrincho* is a sheep's or goat's milk cheese made from unpasteurized milk in the Trás-os-Montes and Alto Douro regions. It is coated in paprika and matured for at least 30 days. It is often cut into chunks and preserved in jars of olive oil.
- *Serra da Estrela*, often called simply Serra, is a product from the Star Mountain region. Traditionally presented wrapped in cloth, it is quite runny and is served with a spoon, with a mild and creamy paste.

The Portuguese love to eat their cheese with *marmelada* (quince jelly), a sweet and savoury combination that goes well with a glass of Port or a Portuguese red wine.

DONANTÓNIA

NEW CLASSICS

DonAntónia (see page 295) was a lovely patisserie in Paris's
10th *arrondissement*, sadly now closed. It was the kind of place you'd
like to see in every neighbourhood: beautiful cakes, pretty gourmet
creations and a wonderful welcome. This little Portuguese paradise was
run by Virginie and her family. Donna Antónia, Virginie's mother-in-law,
took over the patisserie in the Paris suburbs 35 years ago. Virginie then
decided to open a catering business and tea room to share sweet and
savoury Portuguese delicacies with others. Here is a small selection of
their recipes.

TRADITIONAL CALDO VERDE

SERVES **6** • PREPARATION: **30 MINUTES** • COOKING: **25 MINUTES**

EQUIPMENT: **STICK BLENDER**

A recipe that's sure to be a hit every time, filled with nutrition and great for colder weather. No secrets, just great ingredients.

1. Heat the oil in a saucepan over a medium heat. Sauté the onions and garlic until softened but not coloured. Add the potatoes and sweet potatoes and cook everything together for 5 minutes, stirring occasionally. Season lightly with salt and pepper, then continue to cook, uncovered, for around 15 minutes, or until the potatoes are tender.

2. Blend the soup to a fairly fine purée with a stick blender, then return to a simmer. Add the kale and cook for a further 3–5 minutes.

3. Cook the *chouriço* in a dry frying pan until starting to crisp at the edges.

4. Taste, adjust the seasoning and serve the soup with the *chouriço* on top.

INGREDIENTS

4 teaspoons olive oil • 2 onions, finely chopped • 1 garlic clove, finely chopped • 500g (1lb 2oz) potatoes, peeled and cut into 3cm (1¼in) pieces • 500g (1lb 2oz) sweet potatoes, peeled and cut into 3cm (1¼in) pieces • 500g (1lb 2oz) kale, cut into thin strips • 100g (3½oz) *chouriço*, thinly sliced • Salt and freshly ground black pepper

PATANISCAS

SERVES **6** • PREPARATION: **30 MINUTES** • COOKING: **35 MINUTES** •
STANDING: **30 MINUTES** • SOAKING: **24 HOURS**

EQUIPMENT: **PROBE THERMOMETER**

Pataniscas de bacalhau are small patties that are traditionally made to use up leftover cooked salt cod. They are served hot as a main course with salad and rice, but also cold as a petisco, the Portuguese equivalent of tapas. These are traditionally served in early summer, when the whole of Portugal is celebrating popular saints' festivals.

1 Desalinate the cod for 24 hours in a bowl of water placed in the bottom of the refrigerator, changing the water 2–3 times during the soaking. Drain off the soaking water.

2 Place the cod in a wide saucepan of fresh cold water. Bring to a simmer, then turn off the heat and leave the cod to poach in the residual heat for 20 minutes. Drain. Once the cod is cold, flake it and remove the skin and bones.

3 In a large salad bowl, mix the flaked cod with the eggs and flour. Pour in the milk and mix until smooth and creamy.

4 Season the mixture with salt and pepper, then add the onion and chopped parsley. Mix and leave to stand for 20–30 minutes.

5 Heat the olive oil to 175°C (350°F) in a large, deep frying pan. Fry large spoonfuls of the mixture for 6 minutes in the hot olive oil, being careful not to overcrowd the pan (you may have to cook the fritters in batches). Turn the *pataniscas* over halfway through cooking.

6 Drain carefully on kitchen paper and serve immediately; at DonAntónia, these were served with tomato rice and a tomato and lettuce salad.

CHEF'S NOTE
You can also serve pataniscas *cold as an aperitif.*

INGREDIENTS
500g (1lb 2oz) salt cod fillets • 4 eggs • 100g (3½oz) plain flour • 250ml (9fl oz) milk •
1 onion, finely chopped • Small bunch of chopped flat-leaf parsley leaves • 200ml (7fl oz/
⅓ pint) olive oil • Salt and freshly ground black pepper

QUEIJADAS

MAKES **10** • PREPARATION: **20 MINUTES** • COOKING: **30 MINUTES**

EQUIPMENT: **10 SMALL (120ML/4FL OZ VOLUME) RAMEKINS**

Small, typically Portuguese baked custards. Every region has its own recipe, almost as secret as that for pastéis de nata (see page 279). Here, Virginie shares her Portuguese in-laws' delicious but easy-to-make recipe.

1   Preheat the oven to as hot as it can go.

2   In a mixing bowl, combine the sugar, cornflour and flour.

3   Add the eggs and mix again.

4   Pour in the milk, then whisk to combine.

5   Butter 10 × 120ml (4fl oz) volume moulds and pour the mixture evenly into each. Put the moulds in a deep roasting tin, place on the oven shelf and pour in boiling water from a kettle to reach hallway up the sides of the moulds, being careful not to splash any into the moulds, before sliding the tin into the oven. Bake for 30 minutes.

6   Leave to cool before turning out of the moulds and serving.

INGREDIENTS
480g caster sugar • 25g (1oz) cornflour • 40g (1½oz) plain flour • 5 eggs • 300ml (10fl oz/½ pint) whole milk • Knob of butter, for the moulds

PUDIM DE LARANJA

MAKES **10** • PREPARATION: **15 MINUTES** • COOKING: **20 MINUTES** • STANDING: **1 HOUR**

EQUIPMENT: **10 SMALL (120ML/4FL OZ VOLUME) RAMEKINS**

This is another traditional recipe, this time for orange custards. Smooth and tangy, they are often eaten around Christmas time.

1   **Prepare the citrus fruit in syrup:** slice the orange and lemon and cut into half-moons. Bring the measured water and sugar to the boil in a saucepan, then pour into a heatproof dish and place the fruit slices in the syrup. Stand for 1 hour.

2   Preheat the oven to as hot as it can go.

3   **Make the pudims:** mix the sugar, cornflour and eggs in a bowl. Gradually add the milk and mix until you have a smooth batter. Squeeze the orange and add the juice to the batter.

4   Butter 10 × 120ml (4fl oz) volume moulds and fill evenly with the batter.

5   Put the moulds in a deep roasting tin, place on an oven shelf and pour in boiling water from a kettle to reach halfway up the sides of the moulds, being careful not to splash any into the pudims, before sliding the tin into the oven. Bake for 20 minutes.

6   Leave to cool, the turn out of the moulds. Serve half a slice of citrus fruit in syrup on top of each custard and enjoy.

INGREDIENTS

FOR THE PUDIMS
500g (1lb 2oz) caster sugar • 40g (1½oz) cornflour • 10 eggs • 600ml (20fl oz) whole milk • 1 orange • Knob of butter, for the moulds

FOR THE CITRUS FRUIT IN SYRUP
1 orange • 1 lemon • 200ml (7fl oz/⅓ pint) water • 20g (¾oz) caster sugar

TIGELADAS

MAKES **6** • PREPARATION: **20 MINUTES** • COOKING: **15 MINUTES** •
STANDING: **30 MINUTES**

EQUIPMENT: **6 ROUND, FLAT BAKING DISHES, EACH ABOUT 200ML (7FL OZ) IN VOLUME**

*Tigeladas are pastries that were originally made in convents (see page 277). They are flat
in shape and were traditionally cooked in clay moulds. They are made with eggs, sugar and
milk, and that's it. Over to you!*

1   In a saucepan, bring the milk and lemon zest to the boil, then remove from
    the heat. Leave to stand for 20 minutes to cool.

2   Meanwhile, combine the flour, sugar and eggs in a mixing bowl.

3   Pour the cooled milk and lemon mixture into the bowl with the flour and
    egg mixture. Whisk for 5 minutes, then leave to stand for 10 minutes.

4   Preheat the oven to 220°C (425°F), Gas Mark 7 with 6 baking dishes,
    each about 200ml (7fl oz) in volume, on a baking tray inside.

5   Carefully pour the batter directly into the hot baking dishes and bake for
    15 minutes.

6   Leave to cool, then serve.

INGREDIENTS
800ml (27fl oz) whole milk • Finely grated zest of 1 unwaxed lemon • 50g (1¾oz) plain
flour • 200g (7oz) caster sugar • 5 eggs

PASTELARIA ALCÔA

PORTUGUESE PASTRIES

Our meeting with Paula Alves was a memorable one, and, I admit, it wasn't planned. We were walking past Alcôa, a Lisboeta patisserie (see page 295) in a listed building decorated with mosaics, and decided to try our luck. And it was a great decision! Paula, the owner of this shop, which sells *conventual* pastries – that is, those traditionally made in religious buildings, most often convents – let us take a few photos and shared one of her many recipes with us. Every year, her pastries win prizes at some of Portugal's most renowned competitions and it's easy to see why. They are a feast for both the eyes and the taste buds.

CASTANHAS
DE OVOS

MAKES **ABOUT 20** • PREPARATION: **30 MINUTES** • COOKING: **10 MINUTES** •
STANDING: **12 HOURS**

EQUIPMENT: **PROBE THERMOMETER**

Paula agreed to let us in on a little secret. Here is her sweet recipe for almond biscuits that'll appeal to anyone. The name means 'chestnuts', which they resemble, but we love the fact that they're sort of heart-shaped too.

1   Heat the sugar with the measured water in a heavy-based saucepan and bring to the boil. Continue to boil until the mixture reaches 125°C (255°F) on a probe thermometer and has become a syrup. Remove from the heat and leave to cool for 2 minutes.

2   Stir in 14 of the egg yolks, lightly mixed, but not beaten. Add the ground almonds and mix well, then return the saucepan to a medium-low heat. Stir regularly with a wooden spoon until the mixture begins to come away from the sides of the pan. Transfer to a mixing bowl, cover and set aside in a cool place overnight.

3   The next day, shape the dough by hand into about 20 small, flattened balls, roughly the size and shape of chestnuts.

4   Preheat the oven to as hot as it can go, with the grill on as well.

5   Break the remaining egg yolk into a small bowl. Dip one side of each *castanha* in the egg yolk.

6   Place all the *castanhas* on a baking sheet and place directly under the grill at the top of the oven. Cook until the tops are browned and the *castanhas* look like roasted chestnuts, 5 minutes maximum, keeping an eye on the colour to check they don't burn. Cool and enjoy.

CHEF'S NOTE
These little biscuits keep for several days in an airtight tin.

INGREDIENTS
250g (9oz) caster sugar • 3 tablespoons water • 15 egg yolks • 200g (7oz) ground almonds

PASTRIES

Portuguese pastries are substantial, both in terms of their sheer number and their sugar content. The basic ingredients are eggs (mostly yolks) and sugar. You can then add the popular Portuguese flavours of cinnamon, coconut, walnuts, almonds or all sorts of other nuts. The best-known Portuguese pastry is *pastéis de nata* (or *pastel de nata*), made famous by a bakery in Belém, a short walk from Lisbon's city centre, but there are stacks of other delicious sweet treats available.

THE ICONIC *PASTÉIS DE NATA*

This globally famous pastry was created in the 19th century by nuns in the town of Belém, now a district of Lisbon. The original recipe has been kept secret down through the ages and remains so well-guarded that it is only known by a few Portuguese master confectioners. Many of today's Portuguese pastries originated in monasteries and convents from the 15th century onwards. As the nuns and monks used egg whites to clarify wine and starch their clothes, there were plenty of yolks left over to create exquisite desserts.

EXPLORING PORTUGUESE DELICACIES

I came across numerous *conventual* pastries in the very elegant Pastelaria Alcôa in the heart of Lisbon's Chiado district (see page 271). There, I discovered a dozen traditional artisanal pastries, all of them sweet, golden and graceful. There were wonderful-looking *castanhas de ovos* (see previous page), *delicias de Amêndoa*, *broinhas de gema*, *nozes caramelizadas*, *pudim de São Bernardo*, *torrão de Abadessa*, *manjar dos deuses* and cornucopias. You can find this marvellous shop with its little delights in the address book on page 295.

PASTÉIS
DE NATA

MAKES **15–18** • PREPARATION: **20 MINUTES** • COOKING: **40 MINUTES**

EQUIPMENT: **15–18 INDIVIDUAL ROUND MOULDS, SUCH AS SMALL MUFFIN MOULDS**

The original authentic pastéis de nata *recipe is impossible to get hold of: no one would share it with us. I did, however, find this version, tested it several times and had it approved by Portuguese friends. So on your marks, get set, go!*

1 Preheat the oven to as hot as it can go. Butter 15–18 individual round moulds, such as small muffin moulds, and set aside.

2 Using a rolling pin, roll the puff pastry out thinly on a lightly floured work surface. Moisten one side of the pastry with a little water.

3 Cut the pastry into discs the size of the moulds. Press the discs into the moulds, moistened side out, with your fingertips, to make sure the pastry sticks to the moulds.

4 Put the measured water and sugar in a saucepan. Heat the mixture, stirring until you obtain a syrup. Set aside.

5 Beat the eggs and yolks in a heatproof mixing bowl. Stir the 2 tablespoons flour into the milk in a bowl, then add to the egg mixture. Mix in the syrup and place over a saucepan of simmering water, making sure the bowl does not touch the water. Heat for 10 minutes, stirring continuously. Remove the cream from the heat and divide it between the pastry-lined moulds.

6 Place the moulds on a baking tray and bake for 25 minutes, until the cakes are browned. Remove the *pastéis* from the oven and cool before removing them from the moulds.

7 Serve the *pastéis* slightly warm, or cold, sprinkling over cinnamon and/or icing sugar to taste, if you like.

INGREDIENTS
5g (⅛oz) butter, for the moulds • 400g (14oz) puff pastry • 2 tablespoons plain flour, plus more to dust • 100ml (3½fl oz) water • 300g (10½oz) caster sugar • 2 eggs • 6 egg yolks • 500ml (18fl oz) whole milk • 2 teaspoons ground cinnamon (optional) • 2 teaspoons icing sugar (optional)

KASUTERA

CAKES AND PUDDINGS

Ingrid Correia welcomed us into her little Japanese-inspired kingdom in the heart of Portugal. Her signature cake, the *castella*, is a sponge that was taken to Japan on the Portuguese caravels in the 15th century and left behind in the Land of the Rising Sun. It has been given a new lease of life by this pastry chef. She entrusted us with the sweet, intricate recipe and agreed to share more of her trade secrets with us, all delicacies she made for her customers.

CASTELLA

MAKES **1 CAKE** • PREPARATION: **20 MINUTES** • COOKING: **40 MINUTES** •
STANDING: **3 HOURS**

EQUIPMENT: **20CM (8IN) SPRINGFORM CAKE TIN** • **STAND MIXER**

A sponge cake which serves as a bridge between two countries with strong culinary cultures: Japan and Portugal. This is miraculously light: a thing of wonder. Simultaneously simple and refined, it is traditionally made using a multi-stage baking method, in a special wooden mould. Here's a simplified recipe you can make at home. As you can see from the photo opposite, you can also make a version with matcha powder.

1   Preheat the oven to 180°C (350°F), Gas Mark 4. Butter a 20cm (8in) springform cake tin and line the base and sides with baking parchment.

2   In the bowl of a stand mixer, combine the measured lukewarm water with the honey and whisk vigorously. Crack in the eggs and blend vigorously until smooth.

3   Add the sugar. Whisk the eggs and sugar at high speed for 5 minutes until the mixture thickens and falls in ribbons from the beaters. Pour into a large bowl. Add the flour in 3 batches and mix very lightly with a hand whisk.

4   Pour the batter into the prepared tin, taking care to remove any air bubbles.

5   Bake on the middle rack of the oven for 35–40 minutes, until the cake is golden brown.

6   Remove from the oven and turn over so the baked side is facing down. Release and remove the cake tin and peel off the baking parchment.

7   Cover the cake with a clean tea towel and set aside at room temperature for at least 3 hours, which helps to keep it moist.

8   To serve, trim the sides of the cake with a sharp knife and discard. Slice the cake into even portions to serve.

INGREDIENTS
20g (¾oz) butter, for the tin • 2½ tablespoons lukewarm water • 80ml (5½ tablespoons) honey • 6 large eggs • 200g (7oz) granulated sugar • 200g (7oz) strong white bread flour, sifted

BROAS CASTELARES

MAKES **ABOUT 50** • PREPARATION: **30 MINUTES** • COOKING: **40 MINUTES**

The ultimate family Christmas delicacy. These small golden biscuits are very easy to make, and would make sweet gifts, so this recipe is for a large batch.

1   Cook the sweet potatoes in a saucepan of boiling water for 20 minutes, or until tender right the way through. Once cooked, peel and put them through a food mill, or mash until very smooth.

2   Add the sugar, ground almonds, cornflour, eggs, flour, grated coconut, orange and lemon zests and honey to the purée. Mix until smooth.

3   Cook this mixture in a saucepan over a low heat until it becomes dry and loses its stickiness, about 5 minutes, stirring constantly. Leave to cool.

4   Preheat the oven to as hot as it can go.

5   Divide the dough into small balls of 30g (1oz) each. Make the balls into long oval-shaped biscuits by rolling in the palms of your hands and put on a baking sheet lined with baking parchment. Brush with the egg yolk while the oven heats up, then brush on a second layer.

6   Bake for 12–15 minutes, until the tops of the cakes are nicely browned. Remove from the oven and immediately place a clean, dry tea towel over them (this will add shine). Leave to cool, then enjoy.

INGREDIENTS
500g (1lb 2oz) sweet potatoes, ideally Portuguese varieties, such as Algarve yellow, scrubbed but unpeeled • 500g (1lb 2oz) caster sugar • 250g (9oz) ground almonds • 125g (4½oz) cornflour • 3 eggs • 65g (2½oz) strong white bread flour • 65g (2½oz) grated coconut • Finely grated zest of ¼ organic orange • Finely grated zest of ¼ unwaxed lemon • 70ml (4¾ tablespoons) honey • 1 egg yolk

PUDIM ABADE PRISCOS

SERVES **4** • PREPARATION: **35 MINUTES** • COOKING: **35 MINUTES**

EQUIPMENT: **FLUTED PUDDING MOULD, ABOUT 1 LITRE (1¾ PINTS) IN VOLUME**

This cake resembles a very dense crème caramel and is typical of Braga in northern Portugal. It dates back to the 19th century and still holds a special place in the hearts of people from all over the country. Ingrid's colleague, Bruno, is originally from the Braga region and was keen to share his family recipe with us.

1   For the cake, strain the yolks through a fine sieve into a bowl to break their membranes. Add the Port, mix and set aside.

2   Mix the sugar, lemon zest and measured water in a saucepan and cook over a medium heat. Add the cinnamon stick and pork belly, then leave to infuse for 3 minutes. Remove the cinnamon and pork and simmer the mixture for 3 minutes, then remove from the heat.

3   Pour the mixture over the egg yolks and Port, stirring constantly. Preheat the oven to as hot as it can go.

4   To prepare the caramel, put the sugar and measured 150ml (5fl oz/¼ pint) water in a frying pan. Bring to the boil and continue boiling until the mixture forms a thick golden syrup, about 10 minutes. Coat a fluted pudding mould, about 1 litre (1¾ pints) in volume, with the syrup using a pastry brush.

5   Pour the mixture into the prepared mould and place in a deep roasting tin. Pour hot water from a kettle into the tin until it reaches halfway up the sides of the mould, being careful not to splash any into the pudim. Bake in the oven for 30 minutes. Leave until lukewarm, then turn out on to a plate and serve.

FOR THE CAKE
15 egg yolks • 250ml (9fl oz) Port • 250g (9oz) caster sugar • Finely grated zest of 2 unwaxed lemons • 125ml (4fl oz) water • 1 cinnamon stick • 25g (1oz) Portuguese cured pork belly (*toucinho*)

FOR THE CARAMEL
500g (1lb 2oz) caster sugar • 150ml (5fl oz/¼ pint) water

INDEX OF RECIPES

ADDRESS BOOK

Almeja restaurant
João Cura
Rua de Fernandes Tomás 819,
4000-219 Porto

Cerveja Musa craft brewery
Bruno Carrilho and Nuno Dantas Melo
Rua do Açúcar 83, 1950-006, Marvila,
Lisboa

**DonAntónia Pastelaria patisserie
(now called Canelas)**
Antonia and Virginie
8, rue de la Grange-aux-Belle,
75010 Paris

Gleba Bakery
Rua Prior Crato, 14, 16 e 18,
1350-352 Lisboa

Kasutera patisserie
Ingrid Correia
Permanently closed

Les Comptoirs de Lisbonne restaurant
Fernando Martins et Malika Boudiba
14, rue Faidherbe, 75011 Paris

Les Saveurs du Portugal
supermarket and delicatessen
4, rue Wolfgang Amadeus Mozart,
78260 Achères

Pap'Açorda Restaurant
Manuela Brandão
Avenida 24 de Julho 49, 1200-479
Lisboa (Mercado da Ribeira)

Pássarito, mon amour restaurant
César De Sousa
10, rue des Goncourt, 75011 Paris

Pastelaria Alcôa patisserie
Paula Alves
Rua Garrett 37, 1200-309 Lisboa

**Prado wine bar, restaurant
and delicatessen**
Carlos Duarte
Rua das Pedras Negras 35,
1100-404 Lisboa

Prado restaurant
António Galapito
Travessa das Pedras Negras 2,
1100-404 Lisboa

Rosanamar fishmonger
At the Mercado da Ribeira,
Avenida 24 de Julho 49,
1200-479 Lisboa

AND OTHER GREAT NOT-TO-BE-MISSED RESTAURANTS

A Cevicheria restaurant
Rua Dom Pedro V 129, 1250-096 Lisboa
*Great restaurant run by chef Kiko. Very good
ceviche and lovely decor.*

Alma restaurant
Rua Anchieta 15, 1200-224 Lisboa
*Chef Henrique Sa Pessoa's Michelin-starred
restaurant.*

Bacalhau Porto restaurant
Muro dos Bacalhoeiros 154,
4050-080 Porto
A temple to salt cod, if ever there was one.

O SoaJeiro restaurant
Rua do Merca-Tudo 16, 1200-109 Lisboa
*In the Santos district.
'It's a good tasca': an expression the Portuguese
use to describe a typical Portuguese restaurant.
An unpretentious place where you can get real
home cooking at a reasonable price.*

Restaurante Ponto Final
Rua do Ginjal 72, 2800-285 Almada
*An exceptional view of Lisbon from the other
side of the river. A treat.*

Restaurante Rei dos Leitoes
Avenida da Restauracao 17,
3050-382 Mealhada
*A restaurant a few dozen kilometres from
Lisbon, but an institution. They serve a famous
version of suckling pig.*

FOOD DESTINATIONS

Bairro do Avillez food hall and restaurant
Rua Nova da Trindade 18,
1200-303 Lisboa
Food hall of Portuguese star chef José Avillez.

Pub Lisboeta
Rua Dom Pedro V 63, 1250-096 Lisboa
*A small bar that doesn't look like much,
but serves great cocktails and good beer.*

Pastéis de Belém tea salon
Rua Belém 84-92, 1300-085 Lisboa
*The place to eat pastéis de nata... Be prepared
for long queues.*

Gelato Davvero
Avenida Dom Carlos I 39, 1200-646 Lisboa
One of Lisbon's favourite ice cream parlours.

Confitería del Bolhão café
Rua Formosa 339, 4000-252 Porto
*The heart of traditional Portugal,
where you can try everything
(really everything) from
breakfast onwards.*

Manteigaria patisseries
Ruado Loreto 2, 1200-108 Lisboa
Rua de Alexandre Braga 24, 4000-049 Porto
*The other famous shop that does pastéis de
nata. As good as those in Belém!*

MARKETS

Mercado da Ribeira
Avenida 24 de Julho 49, 1200-479 Lisboa
*The essential food court and market that
has inspired so many other places around
the world...*

Campo de Ourique market
Rua Coelho da Rocha 104,
1350-075 Lisboa
*A nice popular market, less packed than
the Mercado da Ribeira. Worth a visit.*

DELICATESSENS

Conserveira de Lisboa
Rua dos Bacalhoeiros 34, 1100-071 Lisboa
*A bit like Ali Baba's cave: nicely presented
historic shop selling canned fish and preserves.*

Dois Corvos Cervejeira Marvila Taproom
Rua Cap. Leitão 94, 1950-052 Lisboa
*Another brewery that produces some
great craft beers.*

Loja das Conservas
Rua do Arsenal 130, 1100-040 Lisboa
As recommended by César De Sousa.

EMPORIUM

A Vida Portuguesa
Rua Anchieta 11, 1200-023 Lisboa
Largo do Intendente Pina Manique 23,
1100-285 Lisboa
Rua Galeria de Paris, 4050-162 Porto

*The shop that's not to be missed. There are
now several branches where you'll find the best
groceries, beauty products, home decor,
tableware and Portuguese-made products.*

UK/US TERMS

aubergine	eggplant
baking parchment	parchment paper
biscuit	cookie
black pudding	blood sausage
cake tin	cake pan
caster sugar	superfine sugar
coriander leaves	cilantro
cornflour	corn starch
double cream	heavy cream
escalope	cutlet
frying pan	skillet
grill	broiler
ground almonds	almond flour
icing sugar	confectioners' sugar
lardons	cubed bacon
kitchen paper	paper towels
knob of butter	pat of butter
piping bag	pastry bag
plain chocolate	dark chocolate
plain flour	all-purpose flour
prawns	shrimp
pudding mould	heatproof ceramic bowl
ring mould	ring pan
roasting tin	roasting pan
single cream	light cream
starter	appetizer
strong white bread flour	white bread flour
tea towel	dish towel
wholemeal	wholewheat

ACKNOWLEDGEMENTS

My utmost and sincere thanks go to Catherine Talec and Céline LeLamer for entrusting and honouring me with this project. It's been a few years since we last worked together and I am absolutely delighted to be able to bring this book, dedicated to Portuguese cuisine, to life alongside the Hachette Pratique team. Thanks also to the art team and to Claire and Marc for their careful proofreading. I am grateful to the lovely, energetic Johanna Rodrigues for her constant support.

Now to Nicolas Lobbestaël, my partner on this project. We have explored behind the scenes of Portuguese cuisine together, through our many encounters and wanderings. It was a real pleasure to share all this with you.

I'd like to extend my warmest thanks to everyone involved in this adventure: Ricardo, César, Tiago, Rita, André, Tiago, Rosa, Manuela, Maria, Ricardo, Diogo, Bruno, Nuno, Ines and Barbara, Carlos, João, Henrique, António, Paula and Johanna, Virginie, Ines and Bruno, Fernando and Malika and all their teams. Thank you to the Saveurs du Portugal store in Achères, without whom these beautiful photos would not have been possible. I have no doubt forgotten some people, but they all have my warmest thoughts. Their hospitality and kindness were what made this gastronomic tour successful. Everyone who shared a moment of their daily lives with us, graciously welcoming us for a few hours and sharing their knowledge, their stories, their recommendations and great advice. *Muito Obrigado*.

To all my professional contacts and friends who, from near or far, followed the progress of the project and its successful completion. I'm thinking of my husband Johan, who believed in this project since the first day. Not forgetting my sister, my parents, my friends Caroline, Emilie, Amélie, Vanessa, Olga, Magali, Aurore, Gabrielle, Joséphine, Patricia and my former colleagues in Valence who have heard a lot about this book too!

Huge thanks also to Farou and Joséphine for their administrative support.

Finally, a friendly thought for Nicolas Chatenier, who introduced me to Catherine Talec.

Anaïs

Thank you, yes... but where to start? There's so much to say about a journey that's been so unforgettable.

I hope the pictures manage to convey all the emotions and sensations we felt while making this book.

Of course, a huge thank you to Céline and Catherine for putting their trust in me. Thank you for this incredible adventure.

Thank you, Anaïs. Thank you for your kindness, your good humour and your unfailing professionalism. And what can I say about your talents as a model? Sharing this journey with you was an immense pleasure. Can't wait for the next one...

Thank you to all the people we met in France and Portugal: their hospitality, kindness and above all their passion for their professions were an incredible source of inspiration and enrichment. Thank you!

And finally, thank you to the woman who shares my life and who has been a constant support.

Nicolas

First published in Great Britain in 2025 by Mitchell Beazley,
an imprint of Octopus Publishing Group Ltd, Carmelite House,
50 Victoria Embankment, London EC4Y 0DZ
www.octopusbooks.co.uk
www.octopusbooksusa.com

An Hachette UK Company
www.hachette.co.uk

The authorized representative in the EEA is Hachette Ireland,
8 Castlecourt Centre, Dublin 15, D15 XTP3, Ireland (email: info@hbgi.ie)

Originally published in France as *Cuisine du Portugal* by Hachette Cuisine
(La Maison Hachette Pratique) in 2023.

Copyright for original French edition © Hachette Cuisine
(La Maison Hachette Pratique) 2023

Copyright for the English edition © Octopus Publishing Group Ltd 2025

Distributed in the US by Hachette Book Group, 1290 Avenue
of the Americas, 4th and 5th Floors, New York, NY 10104

Distributed in Canada by Canadian Manda Group,
664 Annette St., Toronto, Ontario, Canada M6S 2C8

ISBN 978-1-84091-940-0

A CIP catalogue record for this book is available from the British Library.

Printed and bound in China.

10 9 8 7 6 5 4 3 2 1

English edition
Commissioning Editor: Jeannie Stanley
Creative Director: Jaz Bahra
Senior Editor: Leanne Bryan
Translation from the French: Andrea Reece and Margaret Morrison
Designer: Jeremy Tilston
Production Controllers: Lucy Carter and Nic Jones

All photographs by Nicolas Lobbestaël